Beyond Facts & Flashcards

Beyond Facts and Flashcards
EXPLORING MATH WITH YOUR KIDS

Jan Mokros

&

TERC

HEINEMANN
PORTSMOUTH, NH

HEINEMANN

361 Hanover Street   Portsmouth, NH 03801-3912
Offices and agents throughout the world

Library of Congress Cataloging-in-Publication Data

Mokros, Janice R.
      Beyond facts and flashcards : exploring math with your kids / Jan
Mokros and TERC.
           p.   cm.
      Includes bibliographical references and index.
      ISBN 0-435-08375-9
      1. Mathematics—Study and teaching (Elementary)   I.   TERC (Firm)
II. Title.
QA135.5.M578   1996
649'.68—dc20   95-36594
                                                                             CIP

Editor: Leigh Peake
Production: J. B. Tranchemontagne
Manufacturing: Elizabeth Valway
Design: Jenny Jensen Greenleaf
Cover design: Jenny Jensen Greenleaf
Illustration: Mary Sims

Printed in the United States of America on acid-free paper
14 13 12 11 10 VP 16 17 18 19 20

contents

foreword

Parents today are concerned about their children's mathematics learning, and their concerns are well-founded. When math becomes an elective in high school, more than half the students elect not to take it. This is a dismal situation! Avoiding mathematics in school results in eliminating children's options for a large number of college programs and career choices.

For many adults, learning mathematics was extremely unpleasant — confusing, difficult, and riddled with fear. Classroom memories include the horror of being called to the board and the humiliation of not being able to produce answers on demand. The line seems to be clearly drawn in mathematics, and the myth persists that there are those who easily learn to do math and those who are doomed never to experience success or comfort with it.

In *Beyond Facts and Flashcards*, Jan Mokros handily debunks this myth and offers parents valuable and practical ways to give their children the math help they need. Jan is a parent and a respected mathematics educator who understands deeply how important it is for children to learn math. She has a great deal of experience in helping children enjoy math while they are learning. And she knows what parents can do to support their children's mathematics education.

Beyond Facts and Flashcards offers parents a rich collection of games and activities that help children become successful math learners. The activities are engaging, easy to understand, and designed so that parents can incorporate them into the busy schedules of their daily lives. Along with learning how to do the activity with their children, parents also learn how the activities relate to mathematics, what's reasonable to expect a child to understand, and how to ask questions that elicit and support children's learning.

Jan's passion and caring is evident throughout the book. Reading *Beyond Facts and Flashcards* gives parents a fresh look at mathematics and the kind of math learning necessary for their children's success. The book maks a much-needed contribution to a crucial aspect of children's education.

—MARILYN BURNS

preface

Remember what elementary school math classes were like when we were kids? Each day the teacher would review homework, introduce a new skill, do problems on the board to show how this skill worked, then set us free to work on our homework. Getting the right answer was of utmost importance, and there were many after-school phone calls to friends that started off with questions like, "On the math assignment, what did you get for problem 5?" There was usually a quiz each week, often timed, and the quiz was directly related to the homework. Math was as dull as it was predictable. What most of us don't realize is that these routines taught us very little mathematics.

If you're of a certain age, you may also remember the years when *new math* was introduced. It was much different from regular math — set theory, upside-down and right-side-up "U"s to show intersection and union, and lots of other symbols and ideas to get used to. It seemed more legitimately mathematical than *old* math, but it was hard to understand what its uses were. It was like a new foreign language, replacing the equally foreign language of mathematics in the old textbooks. Again, most of us learned little mathematics during those years.

In some ways, math instruction hasn't changed much. Many teachers are still using the same kinds of textbooks to introduce operations. Most textbooks focus heavily on arithmetic and barely touch upon critical mathematical topics such as number sense, statistics, and geometry. Workbooks and flashcards prevail in many schools, though in the more technologically sophisticated schools, workbooks have been transported to the computer. Children blast their way through electronic times tables, or even do them to rap music, but the underlying approach is the same old memorization and drill.

There's something else that isn't changing fast enough: kids still are being taught *pseudo-mathematics* rather than real mathematics. They're mostly learning to memorize definitions and procedures and are not learning to think mathematically. Despite spending week after week, year after year on these procedures, many children do not know how to solve mathematical problems. Their common sense flies out the window when they are asked to solve word problems. If they can't remember a procedure they have learned in school, they are lost.

As a parent, a developmental psychologist, and a math educator, my mission is to find ways of helping children do mathematics, not just memorize procedures. Like many parents, I feel that my own children deserve a better education than the one I received. They deserve to know what mathematics is and to experience it firsthand by solving juicy mathematical problems. Parents can help to change things, and we can begin by doing three things: (1) We can learn about what mathematics really is and try to solve mathematical problems for ourselves; (2) We can tune into the mathematics that interests our children; mathematics begins with the problems that children discover on their own and decide to share with us; and (3) Above all, we can learn to do mathematics with our children the same way that we read, ride bikes, bake cakes, or sing songs together — with a sense of adventure, surprise, challenge, and togetherness.

My children, Jacob and Erica Sagrans, and my husband, Howard, are as much the creators of this book as I am. We have lived math together. We've cuddled up at bedtime with good math problems, done math to resolve fairness problems, used math to create amazing block structures as well as architectural plans for our fantasy house, and brought math to bear in our informal critiques of the endless strings of commercials on TV. Everyone in our family brings mathematical problems to the table (as well as to the kitchen, the backyard, and wherever else we go).

At work, as well as at home, I am surrounded by creative people who invent, design, and do mathematical investigations. TERC Math Center, which I co-direct, has been developing an elementary math curriculum, "Investigations in Number, Data, and Space," for the past several years. This means that we get to spend long and fascinating hours observing children and teachers doing mathematics. My own responsibility, as research director for the project, is to find ways of assessing how children's mathematical thinking develops as they use the new curriculum. The mathematical investigations invented by our team have been the inspiration behind many of the activities in the second section of the book. I have the privilege of working with and learning from a remarkable group of child-centered, mathematically sophisticated, and generous friends and educators. I'm especially grateful to Andee Rubin, Cliff Konold, Karen Economopoulos, Rebecca Corwin, Cornelia Tierney, and Susan Jo Russell for all they have taught me about mathematics, classrooms, and children's thinking. I also wish to thank TERC's president, Barbara Sampson, for supporting this book by giving me substantial time away from my regular responsibilities to complete the project.

This book is meant only as a beginning. The real goal is for you and your children to discover and do mathematics on your own. I hope that mathematics becomes as much a part of your family's lives as it is of ours.

beyond facts and flashcards

one

Raising Mathematically Literate Children

This book is a serious attempt to help you help your children with math. By now, many of us have learned from teachers and the media how we can help our children learn to read and write. We know that kids benefit greatly from being read to every day and from having grown-ups listen to their reading. It's also important to encourage their writing—of notes, signs, stories, and songs. It's less clear what to do when it comes to math. What is the mathematical equivalent of reading aloud? It's hard to know where to begin, because we have very few models of what parents and children can do together, mathematically speaking. And what about within the schools? What can we do to ensure that our children have richer experiences? How can we help them really like and benefit from school math—not just live through it? What can we do to establish and support more challenging and meaningful math programs in our children's schools? Most important, how can we help our children not only to become mathematically powerful, but also to see themselves as competent, resourceful problem solvers? These are the questions that this book addresses.

Given the school math we grew up with, it is no wonder that parents are stymied when it comes to helping children through math. Our own mathematical backgrounds give us little guidance. Like our children, we seldom have experienced the depth, beauty, complexity, utility, and challenge of doing real mathematics. Let's face it: most of us have been mathematically deprived. That makes it a lot harder to try to figure out what it is we're supposed to do with our own children. What are parents to do? Grit our teeth and make helpful suggestions about how to invert and multiply? What happens if we don't remember how and when to invert and multiply? Before stepping in to bolster our children's mathematical skills, we must take the time to think about the big picture and the mathematical goals we're aiming to accomplish.

What Is Mathematical Literacy?

As long as we adhere to outdated beliefs about mathematics as a collection of definitions and procedures, our children will continue to fail at mathematics. We must help them expand their vision, and at the same time we must expand our own vision of mathematics. Fortunately, there are many resources, described later in this book, for those who want to help their children become truly mathematically literate.

Mathematics educators recently have arrived at a surprising and historic consensus about the ingredients of mathematical literacy. The National Council of Teachers of Mathematics (NCTM) has published a series of standards to establish just what mathematical literacy means and what the implications are for curriculum and teaching and for the assessment of students' understanding. These standards, in conjunction with several major books about reform in curriculum and teaching, make the following key points about the ingredients of literacy:

1. Mathematical literacy requires an understanding that reasoning and using evidence to prove a point are the basic standards of truth in mathematics. In other words, if you don't understand what you are doing when you manipulate numbers, symbols, or geometric objects, you are not doing mathematics. Literacy requires familiarity and experience with argumentation, explanation, and proof as well as the ability to use these processes to solve problems you won't find in the textbook.

2. Literacy means putting less emphasis on learning rote procedures. The NCTM Standards point out that mathematics is being used much more deeply in many fields and in many more fields than in the past. Literacy, therefore, should no longer consist of the "bookkeeping math" that is still the basis for too many American curricula.

3. People need to gain a better feel for the relative size of numbers and how numbers are put together. One mathematician (Paulos, 1988) calls this skill "numeracy," a parallel skill to literacy. Other math educators call this form of literacy "number sense." For example, in order to address questions of budgeting (your own or that of the U.S. government), you need to have a sense of just how big the debt is and how this relates to income. In order to understand how long the earth can sustain its population, you need to know how many people are here now, how fast the population is growing, and how many resources are needed for individual and group survival. Solving big problems, as well as smaller and more immediate ones, depends on having good number sense.

4. Mathematical literacy means that we need to know how to read and make sense out of the ubiquitous data in the news media on issues ranging from crime to the costs of a college education to the prospects of a favorite sports team. According to one report on how mathematics needs to be reshaped (Mathematical Sciences Education Board, 1990), "Citizens who cannot properly interpret quantitative data are, in this day and age, functionally illiterate" (p. 8). Unfortunately, if this standard were applied to adult Americans, most of us would fall into the illiterate category.

5. A growing number of fields require deep geometric literacy: The computer revolution has had major implications for design, engineering, architecture, and manufacturing. Millions of workers are now required to use visual and spatial skills in their daily work. Many are asked to translate two-dimensional models to the world of real, three-dimensional objects. Yet, geometric reasoning and meaningful experiences with shapes, rotations, perspective, and 2-D to 3-D transformations are almost completely left out of school math. As math educator Thomas Romberg points out (Parker, 1993), the one course in geometry that we are exposed to involves the reapplication of geometric proofs established in the third century B.C. (p. 6). While the work of early geometers was stunning, the field has developed substantially in the intervening centuries.

6. Increasingly, mathematical literacy involves the ability to use computers and calculators as tools to solve time-consuming problems. At a basic level, this means being able to use a calculator to perform routine operations and knowing whether the answers the calculator gives you are reasonable. At a more advanced level, this form of literacy may involve the fluent use of tools like spreadsheets for budgeting and a data base for organizing and making sense of information.

A final point essential for parents to keep in mind is that mathematical literacy is not something that can wait until children have mastered "the basics." The skills discussed above ARE the basic mathematical skills your children will need for high school and college math, as well as for whatever jobs or professions they embark on as adults. To be competent and literate adults, children need a much deeper and broader understanding of mathematics from the very beginning of their education.

These are the proposed literacy goals, but you may be wondering about the nature of the underlying problem. What is wrong with our present system and with the performance of our students? Is it simply a matter of deteriorating test scores or slipping grades? That's what we read about in the papers, and it is true that American children's test scores are nothing to be proud of. But it is important to get at the root of the problem.

Why Aren't Kids Learning Math?

There are two basic problems: As indicated above, one problem is that most American children experience very little mathematics other than bookkeeping arithmetic. The second is that even with respect to arithmetic, most children do not know much about how to think. Most children who have been in the school system for a while can do straightforward calculations, but they run into trouble with mathematics that requires much thought. For example, fourth graders are reasonably good at multiplying 359×6, but they cannot choose three items from a fast food menu that will cost about $4.00. For the menu problem, you must figure out that the task involves *adding* without being told to add. You must have some reasonable expectations about what amounts of money to choose. And you must be able to modify your first choices intelligently if they don't work. Most of our children can't handle this level of complexity. As you might expect, many economists, math educators, and politicians are disturbed by this state of affairs. You should be disturbed by it too, because your child deserves to understand at least enough math to allow her to order from a menu. As a reader of this book, you undoubtedly want much more.

The problems American children have with reasoning (as opposed to calculation) show up strikingly on international tests, with Americans ranking near the bottom. While a number of factors make it difficult to compare children from different cultures, there are two striking findings that emerge from these studies: (1) Children from other countries exhibit better performance on *higher order* mathematical skills such as reasoning, conceptualization, and problem solving. (2) Children from most other countries encounter mathematics curricula that are broader, focus more on problem solving, and devote less time to drill and memorization. Taken together, these findings suggest that the deeper the curriculum goes, the better children learn to use mathematics. Another finding from this research especially deserves our attention: the more involved parents are in their children's mathematical education and the more seriously they take mathematics, the better their children do. While many American parents accept the claim that either they or their children "just aren't good at math," parents from many other cultures would find this state of affairs unacceptable.

The problems that American children and adults experience with mathematics show up clearly on tests but are also easy to see in a variety of public settings where math is used. You can see them in any supermarket or department store. It takes only a couple of malfunctioning cash registers to demonstrate the tenuousness of many people's understanding of mathematics. All of us have encountered cashiers who can't make change and those who can't add amounts to get even a reasonable estimate. Many people blame this state of affairs on the ubiquitousness of calculators and our consequent tendency to avoid calculation altogether. Maybe, they say, the problem would go away if we just emphasized adding, subtracting, and the other operations *more* than we currently do. This is a prevalent view about how to solve the problem. But the problems American children experience stem from a lack of good number sense and a tendency to over-rely on meaningless procedures—whether it's the carrying procedure learned at school or the procedure the calculator uses to come up with a total.

There is a growing body of evidence that suggests that these problems are very related to what happens in school. Most of the time, children in many schools are not really learning mathematics: they are just reciting arithmetic procedures. School math, which is dominated by textbooks that have changed little since we were children, focuses almost entirely on these procedures. Despite spending week after week, year after year on these procedures, many children do not know how to solve mathematical problems. Their common sense about numbers flies out the window when they are asked to solve word problems. If they can't remember a procedure they have learned in school, or it is unclear which procedure to use, they are lost. In interviewing children, I have seen firsthand how reliance on memorized procedures prevents children from engaging in sound mathematical thinking. Recently, some colleagues and I conducted a study with fourth graders. We interviewed them as they solved the following problem:

Some dogs weigh 60 pounds.
　A baby elephant weighs 3000 pounds.
　About how many dogs would it take to weigh the same as a baby elephant?

Many children responded something like this: "Just tell me whether to add or subtract or multiply or divide. Then I can solve it." Most children would guess which of these operations to use, and the favorite response was $3000 - 60 = 2940$ dogs. Some children guessed that it must be related to division, and did the division both ways ($3000/60$ and $60/3000$) before deciding which answer was closer. One child figured that this question required that he know something about carrying 1000s or carrying 100s but couldn't begin to solve the problem. After seeing several children struggle with problems like these, many math researchers are convinced that mathematical problem solving is a crucial skill that is not getting enough attention in our classrooms.

I do not mean to imply that the children in our study were mathematical slouches. The children who worked on this problem were getting good grades in math and were viewed by their teachers as having average or above average mathematical ability. It is not that our children are lazy, or slow, or unwilling to learn the rules that are being taught. In fact, the problem is that they are often *too* conscientiously trying to master procedures. They have nothing to fall back on. They have not developed basic mathematical skills in reasoning, communicating, and thinking.

Some readers will still contend that these children simply didn't spend enough time learning the calculations: if they had learned their facts and procedures better, they wouldn't have gotten into trouble. But American students spend well over 90 percent of their time in math classes practicing procedures, and it does not seem to help them become better at mathematical reasoning. It only helps them get faster at doing computations. Our educational system has already clung to arithmetic procedures almost exclusively, at the expense of eliminating other meaningful math from the curriculum. Still, mathematical understanding does not improve. Tests that probe deeper than the surface, calculation level show that mathematical understanding is woefully lacking for many American youngsters.

Even if calculation were the key to mathematical success, which is definitely not the case, research shows that people simply do not remember meaningless facts and procedures. We keep them in our minds only long enough to pass tests, and when they are no longer useful, we forget them. Even after many years of drill, there are more than a few grown-ups out there who have momentary gaps in their memory of the multiplication tables. Deep down, many of us blame these mathematical gaps on not paying enough attention in school and not doing a better job of learning the rules and facts. If you are one of these folks, stop blaming yourself! If your child is having a hard time remembering math, stop blaming her. The rules will never stay in her head for longer than the time it takes to pass a test UNLESS they somehow make sense and are grounded in real understanding of numbers and how they fit together. Mathematics is not *remembering*, it is *understanding*.

two

What You Can Do at Home

Listen to what an expert on children's learning says about parent involvement:

The most important thing you can do to help your child is not to leave it up to someone else. People assume that schools and communities take care of it, but most schools don't have the time or the educators to do it. Parents need to be good role models.

The expert quoted above, Robert Glover, author of *The Family Fitness Handbook*, was talking about children's fitness, but he just as easily could have been talking about their mathematics education. Reports show that children in this country do not get enough experience doing math in school and are "prisoners of time" in the sense that they are bound to the rigid parameters of a school year that is a full fifteen days shorter than it was a hundred years ago. Furthermore, less and less core academic material is presented during the existing school year, and American students spend only about half as much time as their European counterparts on academic subjects such as math. Most elementary teachers spend twice as much time on reading and language arts as they do on math. If you had to make a choice, it might be better to do math, rather than reading, with your child in order to correct the imbalance found in schools.

Does Parent Involvement Help?

A lot! Consider these findings from researchers. (1) The single most important predictor of how well children do in reading is the amount of time their parents have spent reading with them. Time spent reading with parents is more important than the school curriculum, the amount of time a child spends reading in school, or the quality of teaching he receives. (2) One-on-one time, in which an adult works with a child, has been shown to raise average test scores to the 98th percentile (Perkins, 1992). This has been shown with a variety of subject areas. (3) The factor that most critically influences a child's participation in physical activities is the mother's and father's own activity patterns (Lutter, 1990). Parents' expectations for their children also influenced children's participation in sports in a positive direction.

Interestingly, there is no comparable research on parents doing math with their children. No one has thought to do this research, because it's not part of the culture for parents to do math with their children. But doesn't it stand to reason that there would be great educational benefits? Why wouldn't doing math together be at least as powerful as reading (or running) together?

In the Minneapolis *Star Tribune* for November 16, 1993, there were several articles about children's literacy and an announcement about National Children's Book Week. Accompanying these articles were quotations from local and national celebrities concerning their favorite books and what reading had meant to them as children. Another article discussed programs to help adults learn to read, while yet another provided a list of more than fifty local organizations and several national ones that offer reading skills assistance.

Imagine what it would be like if there were a significant, parallel effort in math learning, with local luminaries discussing their favorite math topics and puzzles, parents learning about ways to support their children in math, and libraries sponsoring special mathematics literacy programs. Why shouldn't we see as much energy going into mathematics learning as into literacy? Why shouldn't we see as much energy going into mathematics learning at home as we are beginning to see in the lifelong fitness movement?

We are beginning to see some support for parents who want to do math with their children. A few of these efforts, and some interesting parent resources, are discussed in Chapter 6. But realistically, parents are pretty much on their own in terms of figuring out how to help their children with math. Fortunately, the things you can do on your own to encourage mathematical literacy are not complicated or expensive. They do not require high levels of mathematical expertise. In many ways, encouraging your children's mathematical understanding is quite similar to what you may already be doing to encourage reading and writing. Let's start with some general principles.

1. Do math with your children every day.

Doing math is like reading, cooking, or playing basketball: you need to do it often in order to get better at it. This doesn't mean sitting down for a dreary half-hour of drill. Catch a few minutes whenever you can during the day to do math. One advantage of math, as opposed to reading or cooking, is that you can pull a little of it out of many of your regular activities. You can also build it into your child's play with construction materials and into their game fantasies.

Participate *with* your child in mathematics learning. It isn't that hard, once you get into the habit. There are many ways you can do this, but the important starting point is finding the math that's important to various members of your family. If gas prices are going up, what does this mean for your family? How much more money will you have to spend for gas on your upcoming vacation? If one child wants radishes and tomatoes in the garden this year, and another wants corn, will all these vegetables fit in the backyard plot? How much of each will you be able to plant? If two children are arguing about sharing the space in their bedroom exactly evenly, making sure neither gets the better deal, how can they solve this problem? And how can the family figure out a fair way of doing all of the weekly chores?

2. Let your child see and hear you doing math.

Your children need to see you doing math as much as they need to do it with you. Yes, there's the obvious balancing of the checkbook. But that's only skimming the surface of everyday math, and it isn't an especially positive model if working with bills and the checkbook is accompanied by stressful overtones. When you are calculating how much tile you need for your remodeling project, figuring out the household budget, or checking over the grocery receipt, show your children what you are doing. Let them see you doing math. Whenever you use a calculator, show them what you are doing and how you are entering the numbers. And silly as it sounds, talk aloud to yourself when you're doing math. For example, when you use different proportions for a recipe, show your children how you are thinking: "I'll need to double everything, so $\frac{1}{2}$ teaspoon baking powder should be 1 teaspoon. Instead of two eggs, I'll need four."

Even if your children are too young to understand your mathematical reasoning, when they see you doing math they will get the idea that this is important business and will want to emulate you. Whitin, Mills, and O'Keefe (1990) tell the marvelous story of two-year-old Zachary, who worked diligently each day with his checkbook (torn-out deposit slips), calculator, appointment book, and markers. He had seen his parents working with their calculators to figure out how much things cost. Whenever he saw this, he grabbed a calculator. He made "pointments" by looking at his father's watch and writing down "numbers" in his own appointment book. Zachary's parents allowed him to see them doing real mathematical work, and just like any self-respecting two-year-old, Zachary tried to copy them!

3. Don't play math camouflage.

Don't sugarcoat math, and don't try to hide the fact that you are doing math. Mathematics is truly interesting to children, and to most adults, once they find out that it involves good thinking, challenge, and creativity. Though you don't have to be pedantic and explain the underlying mathematics of each activity, let your children know that they're doing important math. Don't play math camouflage. Children know when they're reading, and it's a valued activity. They need to know what math really is, that it helps them out in many things that they do, and it is enjoyable. When your child builds a great construction, point out the design features that you think are especially interesting and tell them how great it is that they figured out a way to balance the two sides by putting together different kinds of blocks.

In my work as a researcher, I often find children love the new math activities we try out with them, but they also tell me what they're doing "isn't really math." What they mean is that it's much more interesting than regular math. It's important to point out to your own children that real mathematics isn't worksheet pages; it's figuring out how to solve problems that they care about.

4. Explore the math in books you read with your children.

Pioneering math educator Marilyn Burns (1992b) tells the story about when she and some third graders were reading "Ramona Quimby, Age 8." The children understood that the book was written some years ago. Marilyn wondered aloud, "If Ramona were real, how old would she be right now?" This turned into a project that kept the class going for a whole hour, as children explored and shared different methods of figuring this out.

Math is easy to find in children's books—not just in special mathematical books, but in everyday picture books as well as chapter books. Counting books for young children offer wonderful opportunities to learn how numbers get bigger and bigger each time one thing is added. But less obvious literature also has much mathematics hidden in it. While a younger child is busily counting the kittens in a story about a mother cat who gave birth, an older child can be figuring out how many paws all of the kittens have altogether. Just about all children's books present mathematical learning opportunities. But if you can't find any math in the book you're currently reading to your kids, there's a simple and surefire thing you can do. When they beg for more pages and you give in, make it into a math problem. Tell them you'll read to page 76 and ask them how many more pages that is. Or tell them you'll read ten more pages, and ask them what page you should stop at.

5. Let your children lead the process.

Make a point of trying to do a little math with your children each day, but don't overdo it. Children should be stimulated by and enjoy the math that you do with them. If they groan when you raise a mathematical problem, back off. There will be occasions when children want to spend far more time than you do working on a mathematics problem and other instances when they simply aren't interested or want to stop after a couple of minutes. Let your children lead the process and don't pressure them to do more than they want to do. When your child says, "I don't want to do that right now," stop. Similarly, when you are too tired or busy to play Monopoly or do another math activity that your child wants to do, you shouldn't do it. Your goal as a parent should be to build children's confidence, skills, and enjoyment of math, so that they want to keep doing math throughout their lives.

6. Keep doing math with your older children.

We sometimes assume that the older children get, the less parents can do to help them with math. Parents often forget the more arcane parts of mathematics that are introduced in school, like quadratic equations, or the steps in a geometric proof. But the more esoteric math gets in school, the more important it is that you do meaningful math with your children at home. Children, especially girls, often begin losing interest in math by fifth or sixth grade—the time at which more abstract, often recipe-driven math begins to dominate. At this age more than ever, they need you to do math with them and to show them the range of important mathematics that takes place in your family's life. Children in the upper elementary grades are capable of "what if" thinking and are in a position to work with you on more complex problems. They are ready to understand more about family budgeting, buying materials for a building project, planning nutritious meals, and gathering data for the next family vacation. Give older children more mathematical responsibility in your family as they become ready for it. It will keep them invested in math and show that you respect their cognitive skills as well as their opinions.

7. Value mistakes.

Neither children nor adults do mathematics without making mistakes. Figuring out what the mistake is and how the problem could have been solved more effectively is essential to learning mathematics. When a child announces an answer to a problem he's been working on, try to remember to ask, How does that work? regardless of whether the child has gotten the right or the wrong answer. Nine times out of ten, a child who's gotten a "wrong" answer will, as he is explaining, begin to see the faulty reasoning. Sometimes, a parent can prompt a child along a bit simply by saying "I don't get it about your answer." (Of course, you need to say this when you don't understand a correct answer as well.) For example, my daughter Erica recently read in the newspaper that 24 percent of men smoke and 21 percent of women smoke and commented, "That must mean that 45 percent of all people smoke." "Hmm," I said, "I don't get it. How could the percentage of people who smoke be so much higher than either the percentage of men or the percentage of women?" Erica looked at the problem a while longer and said, "It would make more sense if the percentage for all people was somewhere between the percentage for men and the percentage for women." I agreed, and we began trying to estimate about where that number would fall within the range of 21 percent to 24 percent.

Some parents, and teachers, too, think that *valuing* mistakes means simply letting them go and pretending that wrong answers are as good as right answers. My colleague, Susan Jo Russell, and I have dubbed this phenomenon "I'm-okay,-you're-okay math." This isn't the message we are trying to convey. Quite the opposite! We should be communicating to our children that mathematics is about making sense of things. If you focus on how effectively children have made sense of things, you won't worry about a slight mistake that has little effect on the outcome. When an answer really doesn't make sense, encourage your child to figure out a different way of solving the problem that is more plausible. Don't pressure her for a thorough or entirely accurate solution (which may be beyond her level of mathematical skill). Instead, use mistakes as another opportunity to help your child reflect upon and clarify her own thinking.

Principles in Action

Do these principles sound like New Year's resolutions—easy to make, all but impossible to keep? The hard part is in changing your perspective, so that you begin to see the mathematics that is right underneath the surface of everyday family life. Once you do this, it is not hard to engage your children with what you find. They will usually be eager to explore the mathematics with you. The next chapter shows where one family—my own—finds the math in its daily life.

One Day of Family Math

"Mommy, it's time to wake up!" insisted six-year-old Jacob on Sunday morning. I groaned, glanced at the clock, and saw that it was a mere 6:45. I tried to ignore him, but he was persistent. "I need fifteen more minutes," I pleaded. "How long is that?" Please, don't make me explain, not just now, I thought. I told him as quickly and patiently as I could, "Count up to sixty, *slowly*, fifteen times." "But I'll lose track!" "Make a mark with a marker each time you do it. Now let me sleep!" I buried my head back in the pillow and he was off—at least for a little while—to figure out how long it takes to count up to fifteen minutes.

As this example suggests, family math occasions arise spontaneously, if not always at the most opportune times. On the other hand, it's often possible to buy yourself a little time by posing a mathematical task for your children while you're involved with another important task (like sleeping). Sometimes it's hard to see the math that's just under the surface of your everyday activities. Perhaps this one-day diary will give you some ideas.

7:10 A.M.

Jacob's back from his counting and he holds me to my promise of getting up. He wants to play the piano, but we have rules about early morning piano-playing (none until everyone is awake). In the meantime, I suggest that we read for a while from his current favorite, *Fudge-A-Mania*. Kindergartner Fudge has developed a number of endearing traits, humorously portrayed by his brother Peter, and the one we are currently reading about is Fudge's insistence on counting out exactly 200 Cheerios for his breakfast. If he's interrupted or loses track, he has to start over. What a math problem! Lots of opportunities here, not the least of which is getting some breakfast into us.

"How many Cheerios do you think that is?" I ask Jacob. We talk about whether 200 Cheerios might fill one of our small bowls, or maybe a regular-sized bowl, or perhaps even a mixing bowl. He doesn't think it's that many. We start to find out, and sure enough, he loses track, just like Fudgie. Maybe we could put them in groups somehow, I suggest. He wants to put them on a piece of paper and circle every group of 50. I think he's chosen 50 because he told me a couple of days ago that he knows that 50 plus 50 is 100. It's a good number for him to work with, but many other numbers would work fine too. Multiples of ten are especially good because they give kids a sense of how our number system works. Jacob ends up with four circles of 50 (more or less—I didn't count them), which he announces is 200, and then dumps them into one small bowl. I get out the milk, but he tells me he wants a different kind of cereal instead. Sometimes math can be eaten and sometimes not.

The mathematics of this problem goes beyond counting and keeping track, though these are critical pieces of the problem. Estimation is a very important piece. Just how many is 200 and how much space will it fill? Understanding the relationship between size and number is important—and involves both numerical and visual-spatial skills. Keeping track of 200 easily becomes a problem involving composition/decomposition of number. 200 is much easier to keep track of if you break it down. But when the number is broken into groups, the problem involves addition as well as counting. While grouping simplifies the problem, it involves a cognitive leap. Preschoolers and kindergarteners would do well simply to count out the quantity and estimate how much space it might take up. Working with number groupings is an added attraction (pun intended!).

7:45 A.M.

Ten-year-old Erica is up and picks up the morning paper. She dives right into the coupons, as she does every Sunday. We have an ongoing deal: Erica goes through our grocery list each week and searches for coupons that match the items we need. She's also free to make suggestions for things to add to the list (we have veto power). When she's collected her coupons, she figures out what the total savings will be. This isn't as straightforward as it sounds, since our supermarket doubles the coupon's value on any coupon less than $1. She's grown to like those rare $.75 coupons a lot more than the $1 coupons, because she knows they'll save us more. Using a calculator at times and relying on mental calculation at other times, Erica figures our total savings. She knows to double-check to make sure that she hasn't overlooked the doubling of a coupon or hasn't accidentally missed one. In return for her efforts, we give her half of the amount that we save—an amount that she figures out herself. As she gets older, we may increase the amount to 60 percent or perhaps to two thirds, to give her experience with more difficult fractions and other ways of looking at fractional quantities.

Real mathematics is usually more demanding than textbook math. Organizing this complex problem into items that need to be doubled and items that don't demands good keeping-track strategies. At some point in this process, children often learn that doubling the individual items, followed by adding, gives the same amount as adding the items to get a total, then doubling the total. This is a key mathematical discovery, one that is much more powerful and memorable than learning to recite the rule about commutivity. Adding, keeping track, figuring out a way to check your work, and figuring out how to determine a fraction of a total are just a few of the mathematical skills involved in this problem.

10:00 A.M.

It's going to be one of those days: grocery shopping, housework, a gymnastics meet for Erica—anything but restful. We plan our day. I'll take Erica to her meet while my husband, Howard, does the grocery shopping with Jacob. Then we'll do as much housework as we can stand, have one of our few complete dinners of the week, and collapse.

10:15 A.M.

I set off for the meet with Erica. Besides the usual apprehensions, she has a new one: we're low on gas. She notices the gauge getting lower and wonders if we'll have enough to get to the meet without stopping to refuel. Do we need to waste time stopping for gas? I know we have enough, but this is a good chance for her to figure it out. I show her the markings on the gauge—the fractions $\frac{3}{4}$, $\frac{1}{2}$, and $\frac{1}{4}$, and the tick marks in between, which she figures out are eighths. She sees that we have an eighth of a tank left. This is a good discovery—and an important one for a child who's just beginning to learn about fractions. Erica has done some work with fractions, so I push her a little further: I know that our gas tank holds 20 gallons. About how much gas do we have, given that we have an eighth of a tank? She figures this out by saying that half of 20 is 10, then take half again and you've got 5. That's a fourth. You need half of 5 to get an eighth. That's a little harder but not impossible, and she figures it's $2\frac{1}{2}$.

Notice that the school format for this problem is to multiply 20 x $\frac{1}{8}$. She's not ready to do it that way—nor should she! Her method shows the mathematical relationships between the fractions. It works well; it makes sense to her and to me.

Maybe I should have stopped there, but I persisted and gave Erica a bit more information than she bargained for. I told her we usually can drive 20 miles for each gallon of gas. Rather than doing the math involved to figure out how many more miles we could drive, she announced that we'd easily get there without stopping for gas. I agreed, given that we had only 10 miles to go. Sometimes, it's good to learn that you don't have to solve a problem all the way in order to get an answer that you need!

10:30 A.M.

Erica's been quiet for a while, and I ask her how she thinks she'll do today. She's concerned about whether she'll get above 31—the score you need to progress to the next level. She's already made it once (with a 31.25) but her coach wants to see her do it again in order to build her confidence. Last week, the coach said he thought she could get a 9.0 on bars—but Erica thinks she'll probably only get 8.5. There are three other events, each with a possible score of 10. None of her scores on these three events is likely to be as good as her score on bars. Will she make 31? We spent a few minutes discussing possible combinations of scores. Here's some of the dialogue:

Jan: What do you think your lowest will be?
Erica: The vault judge is supposed to be really strict. Todd says she scores low, so not to be surprised. I usually can get close to 8 on that, but maybe it will be 7.5 with the mean judge.
Jan: She's probably not mean—just scores low. How about other events?
Erica: I don't know. I got a 7.8 on beam last time, but if I don't get my cartwheel it could be much lower. Maybe I'll get 7.5 on that too.
Jan: And floor?
Erica: I'm doing better with tumbling. I think I can get an 8.
Jan: So what would happen if all of your predictions were right? Would you get 31?

Erica: Let's see. The two lowest might be 7.5, so together that
would be 15. Then I'd need 16 more to get 31. We said
maybe 8.5 on bars and 8 on floor. That's more than 16, it's 16
and a half. So I'd get 31.5 if I do as well as I thought. Mom?
Jan: Yes?
Erica: The coach said we're not supposed to try to figure out how
well we're going to do—He said it's too much pressure.
Jan: Oh. Okay.

_____

Besides being a great sport, gymnastics is mathematically interesting. It's especially good for children in fourth, fifth, or sixth
grade who are working with decimals and fractions. Notice how
Erica is using decimals to figure out how low or high she might
score. She knows that a somewhat lower score than what she
got last time might be .3 lower. She doesn't want to be overly
optimistic regarding her bar performance, so she discounts her
coach's prediction by .5. These are very reasonable estimates
and show that she understands something about the decimal
quantities. Also see how she interchangeably uses .5 and one-
half. She clearly sees these two amounts as the same. Research
has shown that a majority of ten- to twelve-year-olds believe
that .075 is larger than .5. I'll bet you a leotard that competitive
gymnasts in this age group would never confuse these two
amounts!

_____

11:00 A.M.

Meanwhile, back at the grocery store, Howard and Jacob are beginning to
battle the crowded aisles. First stop is the recycling area, where they
drop off two six-packs of empty soft drink cans. Howard wonders aloud
how much money they'll get back today. "Remember, we get a nickel for
each can. How much do you think we'll get back for this pack of six cans?"
Jacob has just learned about counting by fives, and he eagerly practices
this skill, counting out one five for every time he points at a can. He gets
to thirty accurately, but it takes some work. Howard doesn't ask him to
figure out how much they'll get for two six-packs.

Sometimes when we're shopping, we take the time to look at prices
and figure out what they mean (e.g., $3.98 is three dollars and ninety-
eight cents), or to search for cans of soup we like that cost less than
$1.25, but today there are too many people. However, since Howard
needs a few vegetables for a lasagna recipe, he enlists Jacob's help in
weighing. Jacob has seen the produce scale before, and he knows that
when you put stuff in it, the basket goes down and the arrow goes up to

higher numbers. Through previous visits, he knows that the arrow tells him how many pounds something weighs. (We only use whole numbers with him, with all other numbers being "in between" numbers.) Howard tells him they need 3 pounds of tomatoes, and lifts Jacob up to put tomatoes on the scale, one or a bunch at a time. "Is it up to 2 pounds yet?" Howard asks as Jacob puts on 4 tomatoes. Not quite. When they are up to 2 and $\frac{1}{2}$ pounds Jacob searches for the perfect tomato, the one that will tip the scale at exactly 3 pounds. He finds a huge one and puts it on the scale. He watches the arrow burst past the 3 and frowns. "I need a smaller one," Jacob states with some certainty. They try a couple more until he's satisfied. Fortunately, no one else wants to use the scale just then, and no one told them that kids shouldn't touch the tomatoes!

Weighing and measuring are crucial to mathematical development. Children need to learn how numbers connect with heaviness, to establish that higher numbers mean greater weights. Weighing also gives them a chance to develop their number sense. How many tomatoes make the scale go from 2 to 3? Does the size of the tomato matter? How? For young children, it is crucial—but difficult—to understand that several small objects weigh the same as fewer heavier objects. Weighing also provides an opportunity to use lots of good mathematical phrases, like *more than*, *less than*, *almost*, and *exactly*. Using these words in context gives children a rich and meaningful mathematical vocabulary.

2:00 P.M.

Home again. Erica is happy with her score—a 31.8. She's even in a good enough mood to offer to help with the cleaning. Great, because it's time to scrub the kitchen floor, a task that seems about as unmathematical as you can get. Turns out that I'm wrong about that. Jacob wants to help with the floor (which of course means I'll have to wash his part again later), but it also means that we have to figure out how each child can wash a fair share of the floor. A perfect Tom Sawyer math problem! It's also a chance to think about area, which most children don't do nearly enough of in school.

Our kitchen floor is a black and white checkerboard of 12-inch squares, squares that are great for counting. This makes it possible for a younger child to enter the discussion about what would be fair. Jacob thinks he should wash all the black squares and that his sister should get the white ones. While he's on the right track, I explain, his idea isn't quite practical. Maybe there's a different way of dividing up the squares?

First we have to find out how many there are, suggests Erica. It's a good idea and one that Jacob can implement. He walks across the floor, careful to make each step land on a new tile, and counts the steps (tiles) as he walks. We don't bother with the pieces of tiles, only the whole tiles. When he gets to the table he crawls under it and continues counting by putting his hands on each tile. He counts a total of 126 tiles. Erica double-checks and finds it's really 132, but we decide to go with Jacob's count (he's very proud of it, and his sister's old enough to understand that accuracy doesn't always matter as much as people's feelings).

How will we determine half in a reasonable way? This is a job for Erica. She figures out half of 126 by first figuring half of 100, then adding to that number half of 26. Good, simple strategy. Getting to 63 is easy. Now we have to figure out which part of the floor that will be. Erica notices that one part of the floor has 8 squares per row. "If it was 64, then I'd just wash 8 rows," she states. We call it close enough and mark the boundary with a string. Jacob insists on doing his part first, and we all go along with him. After all, he gets the part under the table!

Notice that although Erica can do much more of this task than Jacob can, we still do a lot of our mathematical figuring out in front of Jacob. Even though he can't completely understand the reasoning, he knows that we're using math to find out how much half of 126 is. Furthermore, he keeps getting exposed to the idea that grown-ups and big kids really use math, and he expects that he will do this too!

4:00 P.M.

Why is it always right after washing the floor that the kids want to cook? Jacob wants to make "Lighthouse Brownies," his favorite recipe from *The Boxcar Children Cookbook*. At least it's an easy enough recipe, usually without too much spillage. He gets to do the measuring, helping to find the $\frac{1}{2}$ teaspoon measure, and points out where $\frac{3}{4}$ cup is on the glass measuring cup. I ask him to find the spoon that says "1 teaspoon." "How many of these $\frac{1}{2}$ teaspoons do you think it would take to fill 1 teaspoon?" I ask him, curious to know what he knows about one-half in a measuring situation as well as a floor-washing situation. Instead of answering my question, he points to the $\frac{1}{2}$ and asks me why they write one-half "one slash two." I'm not sure what to answer, but Erica pipes in and says that it just means if you have two parts, then one-half is one of the parts. "Oh," says Jacob, "then there ought to be two of these spoons that make one of the 1 teaspoon." He tries it by filling up the 1 teaspoon with two $\frac{1}{2}$ teaspoons of flour and is delighted to learn that his idea works.

Meanwhile, Erica is slightly grossed out to find that the recipe calls for one-half cup of butter. She knows that butter is all fat, and she's trying to eat healthfully. On the box, she sees that there are 35 calories in one teaspoon of butter. She asks how many teaspoons in a tablespoon, and I tell her. She's quiet for a while, and then announces, "We're putting over 800 calories of butter into this recipe!" It is a rather disgusting thought, I admit. She looks at the square pan we put the brownies in, knowing that we only get a yield of nine small brownies. "We might as well each just cut off a tablespoon of butter and eat it. That's what they had to do on the journey across Antarctica that I was just reading about." I told her I'd rather eat my butter disguised in brownies. In the end, we decide to reduce the amount of butter.

Recipes provide a perfect opportunity to work with measuring and fractions. In this case, Jacob is trying to link up his knowledge of one-half with the unfamiliar notation $\frac{1}{2}$. It is important for children to encounter what we write when we say "one-half," just as they learn how to write other words. We didn't explore three-fourths in this instance, although next time we make the recipe I may give him a one-fourth cup measure and ask him to make three-fourths with it. Cooking and baking also offer lots of possibilities for talking about ingredients, grams of sugar and fat, caloric content, and what advertisers choose to put on a label. Erica later told me that she thought the butter makers chose to provide the amount of calories in one teaspoon, even though the main markings on the butter stick are in tablespoons, because people would be happier if they thought that a serving of butter was only 35 calories. It didn't fool her! Children in the upper elementary grades are often very interested in "truth in labeling" and are quite helpful in ferreting out products that are low in fat, sugar, or salt. Better math through better nutrition.

7:30 P.M.

Game time. Jacob either wants to play store or Monopoly Junior. He's more interested in making a store, but I choose Monopoly because I'm tired. As we roll the dice again and again, I notice that he doesn't have to count the dots on the dice anymore. He rolls a six and immediately announces it. "How did you know it was six so fast?" I ask. "It's two lines of three, and three plus three is six." Good answer. Just last year he had to count the number each time. There's been another change recently: he anticipates where he's going to land before he actually moves his piece; he's making the jumps in his head, a kind of mental arithmetic that's important to develop.

At the end of the game, Jacob counts his money, then asks if he can count mine. "Fine, but I'm double-checking," I inform him. "When an answer's important, I always like to double-check. Like when I want to find out if I have enough money in my checkbook to buy something, I try to add it up on the calculator and also add it up in my head. If the answers come out the same, I'm pretty sure I'm right." Jacob counts carefully and accurately, first by adding up the biggest denominations (fives), then adding on the smaller ones. He does it with his fingers and by counting aloud. It's clearly something he enjoys, because when he has finished counting his and my money, he decides to count all the money in the entire game! "That's a lot of money to count," I say. "Do you want me to help you keep track?" He ignores me and starts counting. I know he's likely to be pretty frustrated when he loses track, so I just sit silently by and remember the numbers he's saying. When he does lose track, he asks, "What was that number I was just on?" I tell him but don't offer any more advice. A couple of times in this process, Jacob makes a minor counting error. I do not correct him.

Games are intense business for children in the early elementary grades. They are also often filled with mathematics. Any game that involves moving on a board involves a sort of continuous number line, one on which players add and subtract values on each turn. Monopoly-type games are excellent for counting and adding because of the purchasing of property and accumulation of money. (Yes, it may be a little too materialistic for some, but I'm willing to compromise if the math is good.) The important thing about Jacob's play is how much he's eager to do by himself and how he initiates new and demanding counting tasks. Young children love to count and then to add. Try not to correct them unless they ask for help. If they get stuck on moving from 79 to 80, you'll know by the tone of their voice whether or not they want your help.

Another thing you may have noticed about Jacob's and my interaction: I gave a little advice on how I do math. That's about as long as I ever talk math at Jacob, because he tunes out after a couple of sentences, but I let him know that I'm as serious about counting accurately as he is. I suggest double-checking as a way to make sure, so that he'll know that option's available. He needs to know that he can check on his answers himself, without his mom or dad telling him if he's right or wrong.

Math in Life

We did not sit down and do math together today, but it was a very full mathematical day. The opportunities are there in almost anything you do with your child from reading to washing floors. You just have to find the mathematics and raise a simple question or two to highlight it for your children. If they pick up on it, fine. If not, don't push them. The problem solving should seem a natural part of your everyday life. If your child groans and says, "Oh, no, there she goes again," it's a sure sign you need to back off and forget the math in favor of having some other kind of fun. But as you become more familiar with putting math into your day, it's more likely that your children will raise mathematical questions that push *you* further than your mathematical interest or skills allow you to go. If this happens, feel free to say that you don't know how to solve a problem, but that you'd like to work on it with your child, a friend, or your spouse. Show that you're interested in math and that you aren't panicked when you can't immediately come up with an answer. The enjoyment and challenge of mathematics comes in doing it, not in the answer. Model this for your child as much as you can.

math, day in and day out

Introduction

You've read about how one family does math during the course of a day. But it's still far from obvious how to incorporate math into a family's busy life. The opportunities may be lurking everywhere, but most of the time they're hiding. Bringing them out into the open is what this section is all about. You'll find a variety of everyday contexts for doing mathematics, as well as suggestions for how to draw out the math. These are by no means the only situations that involve math—just a few examples to get you started. Remember to start slowly, rather than jumping in with an overwhelming number of math activities. Let your child's level of enthusiasm be your guide.

Materials

You don't need much equipment in order to do math with your children. The main materials are things you already have in your home, including pencil and scrap paper, things to count with (pennies or macaronis are great), and a few measuring tools. The other item that's critical is a calculator. You probably have one, but if not, get a simple one with big keys that children can manipulate. Encourage children to use calculators for any problems they'd like. This way, they'll figure out what the tool is good for, when it's faster to figure it out in their heads, and what they have to know to check the calculator.

Some families like to assemble all of their math materials in one place, so that children can easily select what they need to solve a problem. This is an excellent idea. A basic math kit might contain the following tools and materials:

- counters (buttons, paper clips, macaronis, pennies)
- graph paper, scrap paper, construction paper

- things to measure with: string, ruler, blocks that connect to each other, tape measure
- small set of blocks or cubes (for building, making models)
- a calculator
- scissors, glue, tape, and other construction materials
- play money
- writing materials

Although these are not necessary, you may want to purchase some special math "manipulatives," such as connecting cubes or blocks that make patterns. These aren't needed for most of the activities described in the book, but they're fun to use and are described in detail in Chapter 6.

Parent's Role

The main preparation for doing math with your children is a matter of thinking differently about teaching and learning. You have an advantage if you think about what you're doing as merely an extension of your everyday parenting role. Don't think of yourself as the expert or the dispenser of answers or rewards. Instead of teaching in the traditional way, you'll be teaching by raising interesting mathematical questions, asking your child to explain her thinking, and engaging in discussions about different ways of solving problems. You'll be listening carefully to your child, asking more questions when you don't understand what he's doing, and focusing on coming up with explanations that make sense.

The goal in this process is not to lead your child to right answers. The important thing in this process is making good mathematical arguments, which will in most cases lead to reasonable answers. Your child may need a little help in learning that you care more about the quality of his thinking than getting a quick numerical answer from him. Whether he has come up with the right answer or not, your questions should always focus on mathematical thinking, as the following example shows:

Katherine just had her eighth birthday and is trying to figure out how much older her 35-year-old mother is than she. She's using her fingers to count.

Katherine: I think you're 28 years older than me.
Mom: How did you figure that out?
Katherine: Well, I know you were in your twenties when you had me.... And I went backwards 8 years, so I counted 35, 34, 33, 32, 31, 30, 29, 28. (She holds up one finger for each of these years.)
Mom: And you ended on 28.
Katherine: Yup.

Mom: What would happen if you started at 8, where you are now, and you added on 28 years? Would you be the same age as me?

Katherine: Well . . . if I added 30 years, I'd be 38. So it would be 2 less than that. So 36.

Mom: When you get 28 years older you'll be a little older than I am now. . . .

Katherine: Yeah, that's funny. 28 doesn't work. It would have to be 27.

Mom: You don't seem so sure. Is there a way you could prove it to yourself?

Katherine: (pause) I know. Here's some paper clips. I'm just going to put in one for each more year I'd have to have to get to be 35. (Katherine puts paper clips, one by one, on the table, and counts 9, 10, 11, 12, 13, 14 . . . . 35. She counts the paper clips and gets 27.) It really is 27, because this way is like putting candles on a birthday cake, one more for each year. It has to work.

Notice the mother's role in this discussion. She did not tell Katherine that her first answer was wrong, nor that her second one was right. Her comments all were aimed at getting Katherine to think of a way of proving which of two plausible responses work. The "what if" question that the mother raised was a good one, especially given the fact that the counting backward method seemed logical to Katherine. Many of us would have jumped in early on with a directive response of "No, you shouldn't have counted the 35," to which Katherine would have responded "Why not?" The two would have gotten into a conversation in which the parent was expert, and the child was simply expected to take her mother's word for it. By asking questions, on the other hand, Katherine's mother encouraged her daughter to find a way of solving the problem that made sense to her.

When two or more children are working together on a problem, it's a good idea to let them compare, discuss, and even argue about their strategies. They'll learn new strategies from observing each other. Sometimes, however, you may want to play a mediating role to prevent older children from overwhelming younger ones. Here's an example of a sisterly mathematical discussion, undertaken by six-year-old Jessie and eight-year-old Maria. Their father overhears most of this conversation but doesn't intervene until he's really needed:

Jessie and Maria have just baked, frosted, and decorated a round cake, using a miniature cake pan one of the girls got for a present. They want to figure out how to cut the cake so that each of the four people in their family has a fair share.

Jessie: I think we should cut it like Mom cuts big cakes. We could make lots of slices, and everyone would get a lot.

Maria: It's too small for that. Let's do four bigger pieces.

Jessie: Okay, we could just do four even slices. (She holds her table knife over the cake and demonstrates, making moves that would result in the following:)

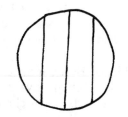

Maria: But that wouldn't be fair. The middle pieces would be bigger.

Jessie: They would not! Not if you make the slices the same size.

Maria: Yeah, but the middle pieces are longer, even if you try to make them the same size.

Dad: (gives the girls paper and pencil) Jessie, how about if you draw your plan so you can see if it looks fair? (Jessie draws a circle and then divides it with three parallel, evenly spaced lines, making sure that each slice is the same thickness.)

Maria: See, the middle pieces stretch out longer than the side pieces.

Jessie: Yeah, it does look like they'd be a little bigger, but I don't think there's any other way of doing it. Maybe we could just cut off the ends, so it would be fair.

Maria: But that's wasting food, and we can't give it to the dog, cuz she gets sick.

Dad: Maria, do you have any ideas about how to divide it up?

Maria: I think since there are four, we could divide it in half, then divide it again.

Dad: Show us on the paper.

Maria draws the following:

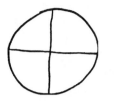

Jessie: I think that would work! It's like cutting pizza.
Maria: Let's do it.

It is not easy to be a good facilitator of these mathematical discussions. It takes practice to learn to do it well and to learn when to restrain yourself. But most parents are curious about how their children think, and if you let this curiosity guide you, you'll be on the right track. Don't worry about making mistakes in the process. You'll have as many learning opportunities as you want.

coupon math

Save the coupons from those Sunday circulars! They are a gold mine of mathematical learning opportunities for children of all ages. Everyone wants to save money, and children can learn math while they help their families clip coupons and save money. You can do coupon math with your children as often as you do your grocery shopping. If he's ready for the responsibility, you may even want to put your child in charge of the family's coupons!

where's the math?

The activities described below encourage the development of number sense and help children learn to compare numbers and put them together. Since most coupon amounts are multiples of five and ten, coupon math is especially good for familiarizing children with these important landmark numbers in our number system. Younger children will also learn more about key number concepts like more than, less than, most, and least. Older children will gain experience with how decimals are used to represent dollars and cents. In addition, they will have the opportunity to try finding fractional amounts of a total. Finally, coupon math will improve children's sorting and classifying skills, which are an important part of statistical understanding.

For all of these activities, encourage children to use a calculator as one way of solving problems. Any time they're working with large quantities or with a series of numbers, a calculator is a very efficient tool. In addition to using calculators, however, they should explain some of the more straightforward calculations, telling how they got their answers using ANOTHER (non-calculator) way. For example, even young children should try adding coupons worth $.25, $.50, and $.75 without a calculator. Ask your kids to tell you when it's efficient to use a calculator and when it's just as easy to do it by counting and using common sense. Talk to them about when you'd use a calculator and when you'd do it in your head.

Getting Set

Children usually know the word SAVE by kindergarten or first grade, but they may not know what it means in the context of coupons. If your child is unfamiliar with coupons, explain how they work and how your family uses them.

- Have your children go through the grocery coupons and cut out the ones they think your family might use.
- With your child, sort the coupons into two piles: those you'll use this week and those you want to save (for math games or for later shopping).
- If they want, children can sort the coupons further, using their own categories. Young children especially love to figure out

which things go together. They might form categories like "junk food," "healthy food," "things you can't eat," "things only pets can eat," or "things you use to clean." It's interesting to see which categories have the most coupons and which have the fewest.
- Now you're ready to do all kinds of number work, which easily can be adjusted to the age, interests, and skills of the child. Your role is to ask good questions and stand back while your child does math. Here are some ideas to get you started.

Coupon Questions

Grade levels are suggestive, but feel free to adapt them to meet your own child's needs.

Questions are marked for their appropriate grade level: kindergarten to second grade, K-2; second to fourth grade, 2-4; fourth through sixth, 4-6.

K-2

Find five coupons that save us at least 40 cents.

How many coupons do we have that save us more than 50 cents?

Find the coupon in your collection that saves us the most money. How much does it save us?

Which coupon saves us the least amount of money?

Find two coupons that, together, will save us more than a dollar. Try finding another combination that saves us more than a dollar.

Find as many junk food coupons as you can that are worth less than 50 cents.

2-4

Do we have enough coupons to save us at least $5.00 (or any other dollar amount) on our groceries this week? Prove it.

With our coupons, how much money will we save on "things you can't eat" this week? How much will we save on "healthy things?" (Use the child's own categories in making up your questions.)

Find as many combinations of two coupons as you can that are exactly equal to $1.00. See if you can find combinations of three coupons that are exactly equal to $1.00.

Which of your categories have coupons with the greatest value? Which have coupons with the least value? What does this say about the things that manufacturers want us to buy? (Do you ever find coupons for fresh fruits and vegetables?)

4-6

How much will we save with the coupons that you've collected for this trip to the grocery store?

Describe your market's policy for doubling (or tripling) coupons. Ask your child to redo the calculations with this information in mind.

If your child has found two (or more) coupons for the same item: Which of these coupons will save us the most? (For example, if we save $.65 on two 8 oz. packages of cream cheese, is that more or less of a bargain than saving $.45 on one 10 oz. package?)

If you'd like to reward your child for helping with the coupons: I'll give you ____ (one-tenth, one-fourth, one-third, one-half) of the amount that you have helped us save. How much will that be?

Following Up

1. In the store

K-2

Find the things that we have coupons for. Find and read aloud the price on some of these items. (Help your child read the dollars and cents notation.)

2-4

As you find the things that we have coupons for, keep a running total on the calculator.

2-6

Once the clerk has entered in the coupons and given you the receipt, have the child check the clerk's "savings" figures against her own. How much was the total bill without the coupons? How much was it with the coupons? What does this mean about the amount that we saved? Is it what you expected?

4-6

About what fraction of our total bill did we save with our coupons? More or less than one-tenth? How do you know?

2. Back at home

Coupon game

Coupons that you don't use at the store do have another use: Save them and play "How much will I save?" with your child (K–4). Spread out your collection of coupons on the table. Then take turns asking questions like:

"How much will I save if I buy toothpaste and butter?"

You can even invent silly stories or "word problems" to go along with these questions. For example,

"Mr. Tai wanted to make peanut butter and stewed tomato sandwiches. How much could he save on the ingredients with our coupons?"

Cleanup

When you've finished, it's cleanup time with a mathematical bent. Ask your child to sort the coupons and put them in envelopes. Or, if you have a coupon filer, have your child sort the coupons into the categories in the filer.

waiting around math

Here's a sobering math question for you: What percentage of your waking hours do you spend waiting to check out at the supermarket or hardware store; waiting for the doctor, dentist, or piano teacher; or waiting for food at a restaurant? Waiting can eat up a lot of time and waiting with kids can be torture. But it doesn't have to be. These spare hours of waiting can easily be filled with mental math that will spark your children's interest and develop their facility with estimation and calculation. It may also keep them from begging for those conveniently located treats at the checkout counter!

Where's the math?

A critical math survival skill is being able to estimate and calculate in your head. This is commonly referred to by math educators as **mental math**. For example, most adults can figure out about how much money they'll need to buy the items in their shopping basket or calculate how much they'll need to pay for parking. We don't usually get out pencil and paper to calculate these amounts—nor should we. Everyday functioning depends on being able to put numbers together well enough to do simple calculations or to get a ballpark estimate of how much our purchases will cost. Children need these skills too and may not be getting enough opportunities in school to develop them.

Spare moments, like those you spend waiting, are ideal moments to do mental math. In the activities that follow, children will learn to combine and compare numbers, estimate how much several items cost, and make predictions concerning how much longer they will be waiting. All of these activities involve using their knowledge of the number system sensibly. Some are simple games that can be done any place that you're waiting, while other activities are directly related to the place where you're waiting (with a special emphasis on supermarkets!). Remember that the aim is to develop good strategies. As you work, focus on how kids are coming up with their answers, rather than the answers themselves. Ask questions like these:

• How are you figuring that out?
• I saw you were thinking hard about that. What were you doing?
• How did you put those numbers together?

And by all means, share your own mental math strategies with your children—not as definitive answers but simply as one way of approaching the problem.

Getting Set

These are truly no-fuss, no-muss activities. It's a good idea to have a calculator and a watch on hand, as well as the small calendar in your checkbook. (I never wait in line without a watch—how else can I complain to my family about how long it took?)

Number Games

Here are a few number games you can play just about anywhere.

Making a Date

1. Identify what day of the month it is.
2. Take turns making up different ways of expressing this date:

Example:

> Mom: Today is the fifteenth of March. That's 5 + 5 + 5.
> Six-year-old: It's 10 + 5.
> Eleven-year-old: It's 3 + 2 + 10.
> Mom: New rule. You can't add. It's 17 – 2.
> Six-year-old: It's 16 – 1.
> Eleven-year -old: It's 45 divided by 3.

Variation

Vary this however you'd like, depending on your child's skills. Older children may like playing a game in which you have to use fractions, need to use at least three numbers, or must use both addition and subtraction to get your total. Experiment!

Making Hundreds (or Tens or Thousands)

1. Think of a number between 1 and 100 and tell it to your partner.
2. Your partner figures out a number that, when added to your number, makes 100. They should say how they are figuring it out.
3. Check on the calculator or have the other person verify.

Example:

> Dad: My number is 20.
> Nine-year-old: 20 to 30 is 10, 30 to 40 is 10, and 40 to 50 is 10. 10 + 10 + 10 = 30. Then to get from 50 to 100 is 50. So it's 50 + 30 = 80.
> Dad: Let's check it on the calculator. 10 + 10 + 10 is 30, then 50 more is 100.
> Nine-year-old: My number is 78.
> Dad: 78 to 80 is 2, then add 20 more to make 100, so it's 22.

Variation

Vary the "target number" to suit your child's skill level. Even young children can play this game when the target is 10 or 20. Older children might like to play with 1000 or even 10,000.

Shoppers' Countdown

You can play this anywhere, but it's most fun to play when you're shopping for a gift for someone.

2~6

1. If you are shopping for a gift, ask your child how many more days it is until the big occasion. You may need to remind the child of today's date and the date of the occasion.

2. Choose a gift-giving occasion that has special meaning for your child. Choose her birthday, Chanukah, or a family member's birthday. For younger children, choose a date in the immediate future. Older children can work with dates that are farther away.

3. Tell her today's date and ask her to figure out how long it is until the big day. Give her the calendar in your checkbook to help her keep track.

Waiting to Be Served

Whenever you're waiting for food at a restaurant, try this: Have everyone who's with you make a prediction about the number of minutes it will take from the time you order until the time you're actually served. (Decide ahead of time what your definition of "getting served" means. Is it when drinks come or when the first food comes? When everybody's food comes?) Make someone the official timer. That person decides the exact moment to start and stop the watch. Once the timer announces the time, the kids decide whose guess was closest.

Shop and Wait

While you're waiting in line with your purchases, try these simple activities.

K~4

Choose two or three items that you're buying. Show your child where the price stickers are and ask him to estimate how much these will cost altogether. For a younger child, you may need to explain about dollars and cents or simply tell him how many dollars each thing costs.

2–6

Start by having the child figure out about how much (to the nearest dollar) the items you are buying will cost. Then ask questions like these:

"If I pay for these with a $10 bill, how much change will I get back?"

"If I pay for them with a $20 bill, how much change will I get back?"

K–4

If your child gets to choose a treat for him/herself when food shopping, ask how much change they expect to get from a $1 bill.

2–6

If grandma gave you $5 and made you spend it all on candy from next to the checkout counter, what could you buy?

How Much Longer?

(You'll need a watch for these.) In many instances when you're waiting, you can figure out how long it's taking other people in line to make their transactions and use this information to get a rough idea about when it will be your turn. The longer the line, the more interesting these questions become.

K–2

"How long do you suppose it will take for the next person in line to _____ (get money from the money machine, check out at the supermarket counter, buy tickets, etc.) ? How could you figure it out? When do you start timing, and when do you stop?" The focus here is on timing different transactions.

K–2

Keep track of how long it takes several people to make their transactions. What's the longest amount of time it took? The shortest?

2–6

Again, have your child figure out about how long it takes for a person to make his/her transaction. Then ask "If it takes about___ seconds/minutes for a person to make his/her purchase, about how much longer will it be until we get to the front of the line?"

Which of the lines seems to be moving fastest? Slowest? Should we switch lines? Why or why not?

2-6

What's the average amount of time it takes for a person to make his/her purchase? How did you figure it out?

4-6

board and card game math

Do your kids love to play board games? Are they becoming regular card sharks? Then they're already doing a surprising amount of math. The activities in this section will help you find and focus on the math in popular games and also help you extend these games in mathematically interesting ways. You'll also discover some ways to level the playing field, in a mathematical sense, when kids of different ages play the same game. Almost every board or card game is based on mathematical principles. Once you've tried a few of the suggestions below, you and your kids will be ready to find the math in any game that you try. You'll also be able to make up your own games.

Where's the Math?

Board games, with their adventurous paths through fantasy-lands of every imaginable kind, are an excellent context for learning about an increasingly prominent area of mathematics: *the mathematics of change*. Young children get concrete experience with step-by-step changes when they are moving their pieces along a board. Predicting where their piece will land is not only part of the suspense and fun, but also a meaningful mathematical feat. In the ideas for game expansions described below, older children will use their own favorite games to build the mathematical concept of *net change*. They will be able to control their moves a bit more than usual by using numbers on the dice as either positive or negative numbers. Of course, this will familiarize them with the idea of combining negative numbers, as well as the concept of net change.

The card games highlighted in this section will help children develop number sense and also begin to organize and understand data. A great feature of card games is that they always include two types of data simultaneously—number data and suit data (or quantitative and qualitative data, in the words of statisticians). Card games allow children to think about what data they have in their hands, as well as what data are missing, and even to think about the probability that they may or may not find the cards they are looking for. It is no accident that much of the mathematical literature on probability is based on card games!

Getting Set

You'll need the board or card games that your child already enjoys playing, as well as paper for scoring and keeping track. There's little to do in advance, and your main role during the games will be to ask good mathematical questions and help kids figure out some age-appropriate extensions. One special challenge is described at the end of this section for board game fanatics—a project that allows children to invent their own board games. If they'd like to do this, they'll need pieces of cardboard, scissors, tape, construction paper, and markers.

Card Games

K-2

Organizing cards. Give your young child a card deck to organize. "Make a system for these cards so that I could find any card that I wanted to very quickly." After the child has finished, ask about his/her organizational plan. Ask him/her to make a different way of organizing the cards.

K-4

How many cards? Play this question and answer game during "down" time in a card game (like when you're between rounds, or waiting for someone to come back with a snack). Lay out (or have your child lay out) the 52 cards in order, and by suit. Remind kids that there are 52 cards in a deck. Then take turns asking each other questions, such as:

- How many cards are hearts?
- How many cards are black?
- How many cards are black aces?
- How many cards are face cards? Red face cards?
- How many cards are lower than 6?

4-6

Play **How many cards?** without laying out the cards!

Reinventing War

2-6

If your children know how to play War, they know that you aren't supposed to cheat by looking at and arranging your cards in advance. But what if both players were allowed to arrange their cards any way they wanted? What strategies would you use to win? There are a couple of different ways, and players should decide in advance how they want to alter the rules:

- Each player arranges his/her entire stack of cards before playing a round.
- Each player chooses the next card to play based on the card that her opponent has put down.

Encourage kids to talk about whether it's easier or harder to play War this new way and to explain what strategies they use. Do their strategies matter, or is it still always a matter of luck?

Solitaire

2-6

How often do you win at Solitaire? The next ten or so times you play the game, keep track of how often you win. Predict how often you'll win over the next ten games based on your past performance.

Changing the rules: How will it affect your "win rate" if you turn over the cards one at a time instead of three at a time? Make a prediction, then keep track over the next ten games and see what happens. Why do you think this happens?

Board Games

Doing it on your own

K–2

For young children, just figuring out how many steps to move is an important mathematical task. Try not to call out the number when a child rolls a die. Young children need experience counting those dots and eventually figuring out what pattern on the die makes four, five, or six. Games that involve two dice are very good for addition facts through the sixes. Watch while your child counts on to arrive at a total, at first slowly and one by one, then with increasing confidence and recognition of some of the basic number patterns. You might try playing some of your child's favorite board games, like Monopoly Jr., with two (or even three) dice rather than one. It's fun to move around the board more quickly, and it gives children experience working with more difficult combinations of numbers.

Counting money

K–4

Counting and keeping track of "play" money offers children a chance to learn to count by fives, tens, twenties, and higher denominations. Be aware of how you are counting money when you play a board game, how you sort it into piles, order it, and count it. Explain to children what you are doing and why. Encourage them to count their money using different methods, including counting it on the calculator. Some children get very intrigued by counting money. If yours is one of them, have him/her count up all the tens, fives, or even all the money in the whole box.

Positive or negative

K–2

This is a simple modification to any game that involves a die or spinner: Once s/he's figured out how many spaces to move, allow the child to decide whether to go FORWARD or BACKWARD this number. Going backward has its appeal in many games, as it may help you avoid the giant trap ahead (maybe even prevent you from falling down that endlessly long chute in one classic kids' game).

Net change

2–6

This is another modification, one you can use with any game that involves two dice: The rules are that one die needs to be assigned a POSITIVE change, and the other a NEGATIVE change. The player gets to decide which die is positive, which is negative. In other words, if one die says 6, the other says 4, the player can either move forward 6, back 4, or backward 6, forward 4. This introduces kids to the idea of net change, and can be made even more fun by using several dice. Just figure out ahead of time what the rules will be (e.g., how many positive, how many negative changes). Rules like this give kids a little more control over where they land and make the games more fun.

Making Your Own Board Game

It's often fun for kids to make their own board games. Just think of the power (not to mention the mathematics) involved in making up your own rules! They'll need to make a path, decide how long from start to finish, and figure out what different things can happen to a player along the way. If instructions involve moving backward or forward a certain number of spaces, they'll need to figure out whether this is a possible outcome (e.g., you can't move back three spaces on the second space of the board), as well as the outcome they desire!

Contexts: There are all kinds of interesting contexts for board games. Children might want to develop games around the theme from a favorite book (e.g., Boxcar Children Board Game), make a popular TV show into a board game, or perhaps use a more socially relevant theme (The Recycle Game). Sports provide another good context for games, as children can incorporate whatever they know about the rules for competition into the rules for their own game.

Inventing the rules: Here are some questions to ask children as they invent the rules for the game. Do you want players to be able to move quickly toward the end, or should it take a long time? What does this mean in terms of how far a player should move on a turn? (Should they use one die, two, or more?) Do you want lots of things to happen to players along the road? Will there be different routes of getting to the end? Will players have some choice in how they move? Will they be able to move just forward, or forward and backward?

Revising: Encourage children to try out different rules or to modify their game to make it more exciting. The idea of a rough draft is helpful here. People who make games try them out with all kinds of groups of kids and change them until they're just right.

traveling math

Where are we now? When will we get there? How often do you hear these questions from your children when you're traveling? It's time to let your children determine for themselves where you are and when you'll get there. Whether you're traveling cross-country or are stuck in a traffic jam on the way to school, traveling presents straightforward, ready-made opportunities for doing math. And keeping kids busy with math has an added attraction: it reduces annoying whining and helps you keep your sanity!

ᴡᴇᴇᴇᴇ's ᴛᴇ ᴍᴀᴛᴇ?

Children's questions about when you'll get there are actually questions about time, distance, and space. All of these, and the relationship between them, are critical mathematical concepts. (Remember the old "two trains are traveling at a rate of . . ." word problems?) When you're traveling, children can readily learn about calculating and comparing distances, and older children can learn about how long it takes to cover distances at given speeds. Traveling also gives children opportunities to make sense of directions, maps, and spatial relationships. On an even more basic level, traveling familiarizes children with units of measure like block, kilometer, and mile and helps them understand how these units are used to figure out distances.

A commonplace tool you'll need for Traveling Math is a map. Maps allow children to see distance in a concrete way, and even though most young children have no idea about scale, they will soon begin examining the length of the roads from place to place and determining which distances are longer and shorter. Maps provide children with a way of developing spatial and geometry skills (Which way are we going now?) and of linking these skills to their understanding of number. Try to take maps whenever you travel, and call attention to and use the maps that are all around you (subway maps, bus routes, airline maps). All of these maps present different ways of thinking about and representing space and distance and are important tools for doing mathematics. Last but not least, encourage your child to make his or her own maps of places you go. Making your own representations of distance and space—however primitive—is a key mathematical skill!

Getting Set

Whenever you travel, take a traveling kit with you that includes these things:

- maps of destinations (including subway and bus routes)
- pencil or markers and paper
- about a hundred or so objects to count with (paper clips, small blocks)

In addition, try to make sure that at least one of the travelers has a watch that counts seconds.

How Long Is It?

1. Stoplights

When you're traveling in the city (by bus or by car), ask children to watch for stoplights. They will study stoplight patterns and will need pencil and paper as well as a watch for this job. Here are some questions to start off.

How many stoplights are there from our apartment to _____?

How many of the stoplights were red when we got to them? How many were green? Which was greater, the number of red or number of green stoplights?

K–2

How long is each stoplight red? How could we measure this? (Some children will recognize that you need to see the stoplight turn red in order to get an accurate starting point. Encourage this kind of discussion.)

2–4

Which stoplights, in which locations, seem to stay red the longest? Which stay green the longest?

2–4

2. Bus (or subway) stops

A route schedule, as well as pencil and paper and watch, are good to have on hand for these questions.

How long does the bus or subway driver open the doors at each stop? Is it the same each time? Why do you think it's different?

K–2

How long does it take the driver to get from our stop to the next scheduled stop? The stop after that? Make a map that shows how long each segment of the trip takes. (This is an excellent activity for children who have long bus rides to school.)

2–4

How long does it take us to get from home to _____ each time we take the bus (or subway) there? What's the shortest amount of time it has taken us? The longest? If we need to be at our destination by a certain time, when should we leave home?

4–6

3. Longer trips

These questions are primarily for car trips lasting more than half an hour. You'll need objects to count with, a couple of containers for these objects, and pencil and paper. One more advance preparation: figure out how far it is to your destination and begin the trip by announcing how many miles the trip will be.

Whenever a child asks how much farther, turn the tables and ask these questions:

K-4

It's _____ miles to the city. We've gone _____ miles. How much longer do we have to go? (Encourage kids to use the objects to count miles traveled or miles remaining.)

K-4

Counting miles by fives and tens: "I'm going to tell you whenever we've gone 5 (or 10) miles. Your job is to keep track of how far we've gone. You can do it with paper or with the objects." The child is in charge of keeping track, and all questions about how far we've gone should be addressed to him/her!

2-4

We've gone _____ miles, and the total distance we need to go is _____ miles. Have we gone halfway yet? A quarter of the way? What fraction of the total have we gone? or, what fraction of the total trip do we still have to go?

2-4

It will take us 2 more hours to get to grandma's house. We have two (or however many) tapes to listen to. Each of them lasts 30 minutes. Which will happen first—we run out of tapes to listen to, or we get to grandma's?

2-4

It will take us _____ hours to get to the campsite. If each of you gets to sit in the front seat for an equal amount of time, how much time will each turn last?

4-6

It's _____ miles to Fred's apartment. Our odometer says 35,265 right now. What will it say when we get to Fred's house?

Estimating time and distance:

How long do you think it will take us to go 1 mile? Let's time it and see. (Have your child time it while the driver reads off the odometer.)

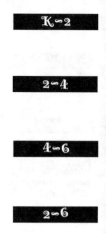

If it took us 65 seconds to go 1 mile, how long will it take us to go 10 miles? 20 miles? The rest of the way to _____?

If it took us 70 seconds to go 1 mile, about how long would we travel in 10 minutes? About how many "miles per hour" are we traveling?

This sign says it's 4 miles to the next rest stop. We're stopping there. How long will it take for us to get there?

Navigating

Whenever you're going somewhere unfamiliar, have your child help you with the navigation. (You might want to do some advance figuring on your own, especially if your child is inexperienced and it's important that you arrive on time!) Navigation involves map reading, paying attention to landmarks, and deciphering written directions and matching them up with the appropriate place.

These directions say it's the fourth house on the left. Which house would that be?

We have five blocks to go, then we turn right. Could you tell me where to turn and which direction to go?

We're supposed to get off the highway at Exit 42. Could you look for that sign and tell me as soon as you see it?

Check on the map and see how much farther it is to Poppersville. We just left Smallville. (Encourage your child to find the mileage amounts from dot to dot on the map and to combine these to get a total mileage.)

How many miles do we have left to go on the highway (on the dirt road, the turnpike, etc.).

2 – 4

I've never been to _____'s house before, and you have. Tell me how to get there.

2 – 6

Write directions for how to get to the party at our house. Most people will be coming _____ (from the west, on the subway). Make a map to help people figure it out.

4 – 6

Moving On

You get the idea—questions like these are pretty easy to generate. You'll quickly find out where your child is mathematically and what's hard and easy for her. Try to ask questions that challenge but don't overwhelm. Encourage everyone in the family to ask questions like these when you're traveling.

sick in bed math

Come on, give the kid a break! Math when you're sick? Why not? When kids come down with colds or the flu and need to stay at home for a couple of days, you need to find something to help pass the time. There are many mathematical opportunities available right from their own beds. Some involve following and keeping track of things associated with their illness (number of sneezes in ten minutes), while others offer a time-filling distraction from their aches and pains.

where's the math?

The math in this section emphasizes recording and keeping track—processes that are vital to solving all but the most simple mathematical problems. Children need to develop their own ideas for keeping track, and they should come up with ways that communicate clearly to themselves and others (e.g., you!). For some of the activities, you may wish to share the idea of tallies—an important standard way of keeping track. You've probably seen and used these before. Just make one tally mark for each thing that you count, but the fifth mark is a slash through the others, as below:

$$\cancel{||||} \quad \cancel{||||} \quad | \; |$$

Children will use tallies and their own representations to keep track of symptoms, as well as things around them in their rooms.

Many of the mathematical ideas in these activities are statistical, with an emphasis on estimation, sampling, and finding patterns. Children are encouraged to count the number of things in a small area (for example, the number of holes in a single ceiling tile), then use that information to make an estimate of the total (the total number of holes in all the ceiling tiles). They will learn that for many purposes, finding "about" numbers—or reasonable approximations—is more efficient and just as useful as finding the exact number.

Getting Set

If your child is sick, but not too sick, you're already set. The math makes use of boxes of tissues, pitchers of water or juice, and the child's own pajamas! The room where the child spends most of his/her time—probably the bedroom, but other rooms will do—offers the data for many of the mathematical activities. Besides this, your child will need a watch or clock, pencil, paper, and a calculator.

Distractions

How many (stripes, figures, patterns, etc.) do you think there are on your pajamas? Count them and see. How will you keep track so you don't lose count?

How many (dolls, books, stuffed animals, action figures) do you think you have? Make an estimate. When you feel well enough, go over and count them. How close was your estimate? How did you figure it out?

How many tiles are on the ceiling (floor) in this room? Make an estimate first. Now figure out how close you were. Is there any way you can find out how many tiles there are without counting every single one? (Encourage the child to make use of the rows of tiles and count by the number in the row, as in "11, 22, 33, 44, 55. . . .")

What's the pattern in the wallpaper that repeats? Describe this pattern. How many times do you see this pattern in the whole room? (You can do the same with bedsheets, pajamas, etc.)

About how many pages do you think are in all the books in this room? How could you estimate it? (Encourage your child to think about the total number of books there are, as well as the number of pages in an "average" book. How can you use this information in your estimate?)

About how many holes do you think there are in all the ceiling tiles in this room? How could you estimate it?

Symptoms

How many times do you think you'll sneeze (cough, blow your nose) in the next ten minutes? How will you keep track? Have the child do it, then figure out how much different the estimate was from the actual.

How many tissues will you use in the next hour? (Show your child how to keep a tally to keep track over the next hour.) Again, figure out the difference between estimate and actual.

We're going to figure out your record number of sneezes for a ten-minute period. How can we do this? How will we know how to keep track?

2-4 To encourage your child to drink liquids: give your child a quart pitcher, filled with water or whatever liquid you're offering, that's marked at ounce or two-ounce intervals. Explain that a quart is thirty-two ounces. Have the child keep a chart of how much liquid s/he drinks each time that s/he drinks. (This will involve some figuring out! You might talk about how s/he'll know how much is gone from the pitcher.) At intervals during the day, ask your child how much of the quart of liquid he or she has drunk altogether.

2-4 Keeping track of medicines. If your child is supposed to take medicine at certain time intervals, have him/her figure out when the next dose is due. For example, if you give him/her medicine at 11 A.M. and s/he is to have more four hours later, when will that be?

2-4 Sleep chart. How much do you sleep when you're sick? How much more/less are you sleeping now than when you're well?

4-6 We just opened this box of tissues, and it says it has two hundred in it. How long do you think that will last you? How fast are you going through the tissues? How many do you suppose you use in an hour? A day?

4-6 A "normal" temperature is 98.6 degrees. Yours is now _____. (Show your child how to read the thermometer, as it is an important measuring tool.) How much above normal is yours? (Children in intermediate grades can take their own temperature and make a chart of how much above normal it is.) Make a chart of your temperature for a whole day. When does it seem highest? Lowest?

Getting Well

Obviously, these activities are for children who are not too sick. They're probably best for those who are already on the mend but need to stay in bed or at home a little longer. Encourage your child to keep any records she may have collected (e.g., record number of sneezes in ten minutes, or a day). Later on, someone else may get sick and want to challenge the record!

conserving and recycling math

Parents everywhere are reporting that their kids are developing a personal investment in recycling and saving resources. There is a growing number of books for kids on recycling, reusing, and reducing the amount of waste that they generate. (See below.) These books empower kids and help them become part of an environmental effort that will continue for the rest of their lives. Numerous mathematical questions underlie recycling and conservation efforts: How many resources are being used up? How can we reverse this trend? When we start conserving or recycling, how much can we "save"?

where's the math?

Dealing with large numbers is the essence of these activities. In some of them, you will be using a small sample and predicting how many you would have if you collected/saved over a longer period of time. Children will be using information about themselves and their families to calculate what would happen if they collected data for a longer time. They will be making mathematical predictions and extrapolations.

One of the important mathematical ideas that comes up in the context of these activities is amount per person, *per* recycled item, or *per* day. For example, American households generate about 3.5 pounds of garbage per person per day. Or, on a simpler level, you get $.05 per can when you return them to the store. It's not always obvious to children what mathematical relationships like these mean. You can't see these relationships, so you have to imagine them. If you have a pile of junk mail that's fifteen inches high after one week, how high would the pile be after four weeks? This is a hard problem for children in second and third grades because they're right on the edge of being able to envision these relationships. Sometimes they can imagine them, sometimes they can't. (Psychologists call this the "seven- to nine-year-old shift," meaning a shift from being grounded in the here and now to being able to think more abstractly.)

One thing you can do to help your child envision relationships of numbers, as well as think about bigger numbers, is to encourage her to record and keep track of what she is doing. If the child draws four stacks of mail, for example, and keeps track of how many fifteens right on the drawing, she is more likely to be successful with the task. But don't tell your child how to keep track. Just ask questions like, "Is there something you could write down or draw to help you keep track of all these ideas?" With a little encouragement, children invent good ways of keeping track on their own.

Getting Set

The materials you need for these activities are your garbage and junk mail, a couple of containers for water, a scale, and the things you recycle.

- If you already recycle, show your child where and how you keep the recycled material. Show him/her how you sort your recyclables.
- If you don't yet recycle, talk with your child about how you could get started. What's one easy thing that each person in the family could do?

Returnable Cans and Bottles

Simply sorting the recyclables is an interesting activity for younger children. Which things go together? Why do we sort them this way, rather than another way.

K~2

How many cans does our family use in a week? How many bottles? Make a chart and keep track. Find a box that you think is big enough for these cans/bottles. How many fit?

K~2

About how many cans does our family use per week per person? Given this information, how many would we use in a month? A year?

2~4

After you've collected returnable cans and bottles for a week, figure out how much you will save when you redeem them. In many places, the standard is $.05 per can or bottle.

2~4

Ask your grocer how much money he gives out, on an average day, to customers who are returning cans and bottles. Then use this figure to calculate how many cans/bottles are returned on an average day. If $40.50 is collected in recycling money, how many cans/bottles were returned? This can be extended to figure out about how many cans/bottles are returned to the store in a week or a month.

4~6

The Garbage We Make

How many bags of garbage does our family put in the trash per day? Per week? Help your child figure out a way to make a chart, or simply write in the number of bags on your calendar each day. Find the total for the week, or for the month if your child would like to record for a longer period.

K~2

Which weighs more, your child or the number of pounds of garbage your family produces in a week? For this one, you will need to weigh and record your bags of trash. Again, it works well to record this on the calendar each day.

2~4

4–6

How many pounds of garbage per person does our family produce each week?

2–6

The average American produces 3.5 pounds of garbage a day. How does our family compare? Do we use more or less than the average family our size? How much more or less?

Water

2–6

The next time your child leaves the faucet dripping, put a quart container under it and see how long it takes to fill. Tell your child what you find out. The follow-up questions depend on the data you get and the age of the child. For younger children, use simpler numbers.

Ask things like this: If the water had kept dripping, how much would have been wasted in (10 minutes, 1 hour, 2 hours)? What if we went away all day and it was dripping? How much would we have lost?

2–6

One-and-a-half gallons of water is used per toilet flush with low-flush models, and 5 to 7 gallons with old-fashioned toilets. Given this information, ask your child to figure out how much water she/he uses each day by flushing. How much does our family use? You might want to keep a tally sheet next to each toilet to record how many times it is flushed in the day.

2–4

Figure out how much water you use per toothbrushing by keeping a big container under the faucet. Next time you brush, try turning the water off when you're not actually using it. How much do you use this time? How much water did you save?

Junk Mail

We know we get an amazing amount of junk mail, but just how much do we get? Is it more or less (in terms of weight, number of pieces) than the regular mail we get? As you raise questions about junk mail with your children, you'll first have to decide what it actually is. Be forewarned that children and adults won't necessarily agree on this. How will you count catalogs, sweepstakes announcements, coupons, and advertisements? Collect your mail for a few days and see if you can develop a definition of junk mail. Developing a shared definition is an important step in collecting and analyzing any kind of statistical data.

Sort the mail into two piles. Junk mail and regular mail. Which is more? How do you know?

K-2

Measure the height of your pile of junk mail. "If every house on our block (or every apartment in our building) got the same amount of junk mail as we do, how high would the pile of junk mail be in a week?"

2-4

If you let it stack up, how high would your family's pile of junk mail be in a month? In a year?

2-4

What fraction of our mail for a week is junk mail? Will you do this by measuring and comparing the size of the piles of mail, counting the number of pieces, weighing the mail, or by using some other method? How well does your method work?

4-6

Next Steps

Go to the library or your local bookstore and get one of the books for kids on conservation and recycling (listed below). These have many interesting statistics that cry out to be turned into personally meaningful math problems. Your job is easy. Read one of these with your child, or comment on a statistic you have found in one of them. Then just start wondering aloud. For example, "The average American uses 7 trees a year in paper, wood, and other products" (from *Conservationworks Book*).

Dad to nine-year-old: So it's the end of June. If you're average, how many trees have you used up so far this year? How many did our whole family use up?

Dad to twelve-year-old: We have about fifty thousand people in our city. If each of them was average, how many trees would everyone in the town use up in a year?

decision-making math

Many of the activities in this book are playful, but the one in this section is more serious and is intended to help you and your child get a different perspective on decisionmaking. The focus is on using mathematics to help your child get "unstuck" when facing a difficult choice. By constructing line graphs to show how their feelings have changed over time, children can learn to consider more data (not just their immediate feelings) when making important decisions.

We've all faced situations with our children in which they are deciding to continue, discontinue, or increase their level of involvement with a school activity, music lessons, a sport, or even a friendship. A child may come home from a class she's been taking for years and announce, "I don't want to go back, it's too _____ (a) boring, (b) hard, (c) stupid." In situations like these, you want your child to make a reasoned decision that considers more than just the immediate crisis or opportunity. When a child has prior experience that should be considered in making a decision, mathematics provides a useful way for examining the past and using it to make decisions about the future.

where's the math?

The mathematical focus is on *thinking about and representing change over time.* Much of higher mathematics is about describing the current state of something, as well as how gradually or suddenly something is changing. Some things change imperceptibly, while others change so quickly you can barely keep track of them. Mathematics allows us to home in on these changes and examine them in great detail, so that we can see how quickly, slowly, steadily, or intermittently the change has taken place.

Looking at and representing change in a *qualitative* way is accessible to elementary school children, and they don't have to take calculus first! Furthermore, it's mathematically important that children begin thinking about how graphs and other representations relate to the story they want to tell (in this case, the story of their feelings over time). It is the shape of the graph—its bumps, slopes, spikes, cliffs, drops, and level spots—that conveys this story. By making and refining representations that are as detailed and subtle as the story itself, children learn to describe changes over time. The graphs that they make, which have deep personal meaning, allow children to experience the power of mathematical storytelling.

Getting Set

There is just one basic activity presented here. Feel free to make modifications depending on your child's interest and the nature of the decision-making situation. The ideal time to do this activity is when your child seems stuck with a decision but is not in a highly emotional state about it.

You'll need markers and large sheets of paper, but do spend some time talking through the issues before you bring out the materials and begin the mathematical work.

The Basic Idea

Draw the outlines of a graph by making a horizontal line (X axis) and a vertical line (Y axis). Label the top of the y axis "+," the bottom "-." Draw a line through the middle to show the neutral point. (See below.) You may also label the axis with words of your child's choosing, such as "absolute greatest" at the top and "terrible" at the bottom. On the X axis, figure out the time parameter you're dealing with and make appropriate labels.

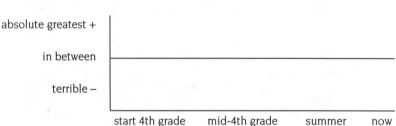

How I Feel about Piano Lessons

Once these parameters are set, ask your child to make a line that tells the story of how he felt about this issue from the starting point until now. The better he felt, the higher the line should go. The more negative he felt, the lower the line goes. As your child makes the line graph, encourage him to talk about and represent the degree of positive or negative feelings, as well as how quickly or slowly his feelings changed. Put labels on the graph to tell what happened at key points.

Some children like to embellish these representations a great deal (even putting cartoon-like captions at various places), while others like to let the line graph tell the story by itself. The following is a fairly typical example of one child's work, but there is no "right" way of making these graphs. Focus on how the graph tells the story of what your child is experiencing.

This graph was made by a sixth grader who was trying to decide whether to stay on her current swimming team or switch to a less demanding one. She noticed two important things about the graph: that she enjoyed meets a lot and that she had a real slump in her feelings about swimming when she began working with a new coach. She was now in the situation of having a second new coach. Last time, it had taken her a couple of months with the new coach before she started feel-

How I Feel about Swimming Lessons

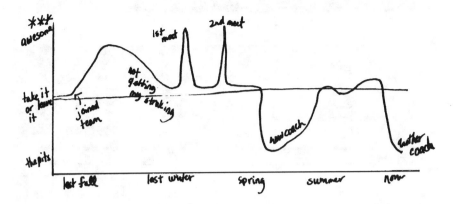

ing better about things. Eventually, she concluded that she might feel better about the new coach in a couple of months and that she would miss the competition if she switched to another team.

This activity is appropriate for children in middle elementary grades (third or fourth) on up. It is excellent for older children and even adults who are in the throes of decision making.

2 – 4

Children who are beginning to work with line graphs will probably focus more on the overall level of the line on the graph at different places. (Don't expect them to think about the slope.) Help them figure out how high or low their line should be by asking them to compare various points in the graph: "Hmm. This graph says to me that you felt much worse about the afterschool program last spring compared to now. Is that what you meant to show?"

4 – 6

Older children can focus more on how to represent changing feelings, rather than just overall intensity of feelings. Questions like this help: "Did you notice a gradual increase in your interest, or was it pretty sudden? How could you show that on the graph?"

clean clothes math

Doing laundry, while not the most exciting family activity, involves myriad mathematical tasks. Sorting and classifying can range from very simple (sorting clean clothes according to their owner) to quite complex (sorting by type of fabric as well as color). And doing the laundry can give you a more concrete understanding of fractions and proportions. The mathematical opportunities associated with laundry range from probability to numerical problem solving. The more loads you do, the more opportunities you'll have to explore the mathematics.

where's the math?

Sorting and classifying are real and sometimes complex statistical processes that involve what researchers call "categorical data." Much commonplace and scientific data is categorical rather than numerical. Researchers try to decide principles for categorizing. (Is this new type of organism more like X or Y? Its structure may look like X, but it moves like Y and has a pattern of reproduction that looks neither like X nor Y.) On a more mundane level, this happens with laundry. If a shirt has light blue and white stripes, does it go with the white or colored clothes— or should it go in a separate pile? Principles for sorting laundry, while second-nature for adults, need to be developed over time by children.

Working with *fractions* is a second focus. Figuring out how many loads of laundry you can get out of a box of detergent is one of the most concrete examples of how dividing by a fraction works. Because detergent, bleach, softener, etc., are frequently measured in fractions of a cup, children have many opportunities to get acquainted with fractions when they are doing laundry. Older children also may begin learning about proportional reasoning as they compare the relative cost of detergent "per" cup or pound.

Laundry tasks involve many unexpected opportunities for problem solving. If you use a laundromat, the relationship between how many loads you are doing, how much it costs, how much change you need, and how much time it takes is the source of many good problems. If you hang your clothes out to dry, there are interesting problems around the number of clothespins that you need. And for solving problems that involve probability, there is some intriguing data-gathering your children can do about right side out and inside out clothing.

Getting Set

What you need here is all too familiar: dirty clothes, detergent, measuring scoop, and anything else you use to do laundry. It is helpful to have a set of measuring cups available for children to examine relationships between fractions. A calculator and pencil and paper are also necessary.

Sorting and Classifying

K–2

Find and pair up the socks that go together. How many pairs do you have? Use that information to figure out how many single socks you have. (Or, do this the other way around: find how many socks you have and predict how many pairs there will be.)

K–4

When folding clothes, figure out a good system for putting them into piles. One obvious system involves who the owner is, but this doesn't always work well. What happens to dishcloths, washcloths, and place-mats? Talk about alternatives for sorting. Maybe you'll decide to sort into piles based on where the piece of laundry is stored. Maybe it will be by owner (with some special provision for items that have many owners). The point is to pose to your child the problem of figuring out a reasonable sorting strategy.

K–4

Explain to your child how you sort the dirty clothes into piles. As s/he helps you make piles, take a look at some of the "undecided" items—the ones that could possibly go into a couple of piles. With your child, try to articulate a principle for classifying these clothes (e.g., anything with less than half white goes into the colored pile).

Fractions

2–4

Give your child a smaller than necessary measuring cup to figure out how much detergent you need. For example, if you need 1 cup of detergent, try giving your child $\frac{1}{3}$ cup and ask how many of these you need. Similarly, how many $\frac{1}{4}$s make up $\frac{3}{4}$s, or (more complicated), how could you measure out $\frac{3}{4}$ cup using a $\frac{1}{2}$ and a $\frac{1}{4}$ measuring cup?

4–6

Have your child measure out the correct amount of detergent for one load of laundry. Ask him/her to estimate how many loads you could wash with the whole container of detergent. After estimating, try to solve the problem.

4–6

What is the cost of your laundry per load? To answer this question, help children extend the work they did with fractions. Once the child has figured out the amount of detergent that's needed per load, follow up with some cost questions. The first is how much it costs per load to do the laundry. After that, you and your child may want to spend some time at the supermarket figuring out whether a different kind of detergent or a different size of your brand costs less. The key to working with problems of this type is to listen to how your child is thinking about figuring out "per" problems.

Problem Solving

What percentage of the time does your underwear come out of the washer inside out? Rightside up? Is this different from what you'd expect by chance? How many times do you need to try this to make sure you've got a fair sample? (TERC colleague Cliff Konold designed this problem.)

4–6

When you hang clothes on the line, how many clothespins do you need if you use two per article of clothing? How does this change if you overlap your clothing (e.g., use only one clothespin to attach two adjacent pieces to the line?). (TERC colleague Rebecca Corwin designed this problem.)

2–6

When using the laundromat, ask your child to find out and tell you how much money you need for each washer or dryer. How many quarters is that? If you need change, have your child work on figuring out the translation from dollars to quarters. Give younger children $2 worth of change, and ask them how much they'll have left after they put the right amount in the machine. Pose more complex problems for older children, such as: "We have to do three loads of wash, so how many dollars worth of change do we need?"

K–4

Which is a better "deal" at the laundromat, filling the dryer up as full as possible and restarting it until everything's dry or using two or three dryers and not having to restart them? This is an interesting problem. And if it ends up costing a little less to go with one dryer—but you have to wait a lot longer—is it worth the cost? Getting children familiar with the idea of weighing costs against benefits is a good foundation for the math they'll be doing throughout their lives.

2–6

reading aloud math

Surprisingly often, the books you read to your kids contain meaty mathematical problems, perhaps even an intertwined series of problems. Rather than just skimming over the surface of the math, take these reading aloud opportunities to "talk mathematics" with your children. To do this, you'll need to think on your feet and figure out appropriate ways and times for exploring the math. Fortunately, the authors of many books make this task as easy as it is delightful.

ẅḥ℮ṛ℮'ṣ ṭḥ℮ m̈ǎṭḥ?

Mathematics can be as varied as the content and plots of the books you're reading aloud to your children. Picture-books are often built around mathematics, and there are hundreds to choose from. (Several excellent annotated bibliographies of these books are summarized in Chapter 6.) Chapter books haven't received as much attention from mathematics educators, but these books are fine sources of mental math problems. "Word problems," the bane of elementary school mathematics, are embedded into the plots of many books. Some are quite straightforward, while others weave themselves in and out of the plot and present many variations to explore.

In the two examples discussed below, the plots are especially math-rich. In one case, the mathematics revolves around multiples and fractions, and in the other it centers on addition, subtraction, and negative numbers. Books like these involve myriad opportunities for mathematical communication. Communication is the essence of mathematics, and books offer children the opportunity to simultaneously discuss mathematical and literary "what if's."

Getting Set

All you need is a good book, a willing child or two, and a cozy place to read. There are many mathematical adventures to explore, and to get you started I've included two of my favorites, *Half Magic*, and *Charlie and the Great Glass Elevator*. What follows are brief book reviews that contain specific suggestions for mathematical questions you can pose to prompt deeper mathematical thinking.

Edward Eager. Half Magic.

In this book, four children discover a charm that grants them half of anything they wish for. It takes them awhile to figure this out, but once they do, they conclude that "all we have to do from now on is ask it for twice as much as we really want" (p. 35). But doing this is no easy matter, because asking for twice as much gets complicated when you're dealing with everything from distances to money to wishing that something existed. (What would it be like if something or somebody only half existed?)

2 – 6

The children sometimes have the presence of mind to ask for precisely what they want, and at other times make hurried or reckless wishes that don't work out quite the way they were intended. For example, when facing a would-be kidnapper, Mark wishes the villain were half a mile away. This is a perfect place to stop reading and ask how far away the kidnapper ended up. Is this far enough for comfort and for the children to escape?

The children's journeys also take them back in time, to the days of King Arthur's Court. This leads the parent-reader to all sorts of questions about how you could use the magic charm for time travel. How many years back would you have to wish for if you wanted to return to the year 1900? How about if you wanted to go forward to the year 2050?

At one point, Jane recklessly wishes that she belonged to some other family. She ends up feeling half herself, half someone else, which led our family to an interesting discussion of what you'd be like if you only had half of your personality. Which half? Would you get angry only half as often or would you get only half as angry as usual?

This book leads everyone to a far deeper understanding of the word "half" and all of its possible meanings. Once you've read it, it's fun to make your own wishes for double what you want and to explore other fractional wishes as well. What would happen if you found a magic coin that gave you double or triple everything you asked for?

Roald Dahl. Charlie and the Great Glass Elevator.

2–6

What could be a more perfect mathematical adventure than a trip to "Minusland?" In this book, three old people squabble over twelve Wonka-Vite pills that are a fountain of youth equivalent: each pill takes off twenty years. This book offers obvious places to stop and do mathematics. Here are a few that I'd consider:

Charlie is interviewing an Oompa-loompa, who has taken one of the magic pills:

> "How old were you just now, before you took the Wonka-Vite?" I asked him.
> "Seventy last birthday," he answered.
> "That means," I said, "it has made you twenty years younger."

Questions to ask:

- So how old would he be now, after he took one pill?
- What would happen if he took two pills?
- I wonder how old I'd be if I took one pill. What about grandpa?

The first question or two are good to ask while you're in the middle of reading, but you may want to wait until afterwards to explore what would happen to various people in your family if they took one or more pills. These speculations make for good dinnertime conversation. Besides, the mathematical adventure has only begun.

We resume it a bit later, on page 118, after the three old people have each taken four Wonka-Lite pills. One of them started off being eighty-one, one eighty, and the other one only seventy-eight. After a brief rundown of the effects on the first two people, we consider what happened to Grandma Georgina, who is nowhere to be found:

"How old, please, was the lady in question?"

"Seventy-eight," Mrs. Bucket told him.

"Well, of course," laughed Mr. Wonka. "That explains it!... She's bitten off more than she could chew! She's taken off more years than she had!"

"Explain yourself," said Mrs. Bucket.

"Simple arithmetic," said Mr. Wonka. "Subtract eighty from seventy-eight and what do you get?"

Dahl makes a parent's work almost too easy: all you need to do is turn to your child and reiterate Mr. Wonka's question. You may also want to ask your child why Mr. Wonka chose the number eighty to subtract.

The book goes on with a dramatic rescue in Minusland, where Grandma Georgina is sprayed three times with a fine black spray that "plusses" her back to existence. The chapter ends with a poetic mathematical problem:

She's as plussy as plussy can be!
She's more plussy than you or than me!
The question is how,
Just how old is she now?
Is she more than a hundred and three?

This is a perfect place to stop and muse about what Mr. Wonka had in mind when he sprayed her three times. How old would she be if each spray added twenty-five years to her life? Thirty years? Remember, she was minus two years old when she was sprayed!

The next activity offers the most dramatic mathematical problem of all, as we discover that Mr. Wonka has made Grandma Georgina into a shriveled 358-year-old. How can we get her back to her desired age of seventy-eight?

Next Steps

Admittedly, the two examples discussed above provide exceedingly fertile ground for mathematical discussions. But most chapter books contain at least a few decent opportunities. In the past couple of weeks, our family has read a Mrs. Pigglewiggle story that had a "fair shares" question (How can you divide fifty pieces of candy fairly among fifteen neighborhood children?); a Boxcar Children book that involved a woman who was trying to bake pies for a living (Would she make enough money if she baked thirty pies a day?); and a National Geographic adventure book in which adolescents were ascending to the summit of Castle Mountain, traveling a thousand feet the final day. (How far would that be in our neighborhood? How far did they travel per hour if they climbed for six hours?) The key is to selectively raise genuine questions, rather than asking dozens of meaningless ones. And remember, while you're actually reading, math is subservient to the story. There's plenty of time for mathematical musing once you've stopped reading for the day.

empty box math

You probably already save interesting boxes for your kids' constructions and art work, but here's another idea: boxes of any size and shape are great for doing counting, estimation, three-dimensional visualization, addition, and multiplication. Anything from toothpaste boxes to refrigerator cartons is fair game. And cylindrical boxes, like oatmeal boxes, add an extra challenge for older children.

where's the math?

These activities pack a double whammy, as they help children connect their understanding of number with their understanding of space. There are many ways of estimating and figuring out how many of one object fit inside another. For younger children, most strategies will involve filling the container as completely as they can, while counting the number of objects it takes to fill it. But how do you figure out the best fit and make sure as much space as possible is filled? Are there some ways of packing that are better than others?

Older children are challenged by finding out a little information about how a few things fit, then using the information to figure out volume. For example, if you know that sixteen unifix cubes fit in the bottom layer of a cube, how many will fill the whole cube? Some children might figure this out by making layers, counting the layers, and multiplying. Others might add up numbers of cubes in each face or side, then count as they fill in the rest. As children become adept at filling simple shapes, it's time to encourage them to work with more complicated ones. For example, figuring out how many toothpaste boxes will fit in a laundry detergent box is challenging for even the most sophisticated problem-solver.

One thing to keep in mind: Some children (the builders in the crowd) love these activities, while others are more tentative. The geometry skills involved in these activities are critical for mathematical understanding, and it's important that all children develop them. It's simply not true that spatial skills are "inborn", rather they result from lots of good experiences with estimating, visualizing, and building.

Getting Set

Collect empty boxes for a while, including boxes for tissues, crackers, cereal, tea, toothpaste, laundry soap, and clothing. Larger boxes work well, too, if you have them. You'll also need some small cubes or blocks, such as one-inch blocks, unifix cubes or other interconnecting cubes, and markers or pencils. For the "design your own box" activity, you'll need graph paper, ruler, pencil, tape, and scissors.

Filling Boxes with Cubes

Have lots of small cubes or blocks available. Choose a small box, such as a baking soda box or a teabag box. Take off one of the large sides of the box to make it easier to fill. Ask your child how many small blocks or cubes might fit in the box. You might suggest that your child hold a cube next to the box, or put a few inside to get a better idea about how the cubes fit. Write down the estimate. Now, ask your child to start filling the box with cubes. When she's gotten into the work but is still less than halfway finished, ask her to stop and look at where she is. Does she want to change her estimate? Make it bigger or smaller? Why?

Now continue filling the box with cubes. When she is finished, have her count the cubes. Encourage her to use counting strategies that don't involve counting every single block. For example, counting the number in a layer and adding up the number of layers is an efficient strategy.

K–4

Once you've completed the above activity and have found out how many cubes fit in a small box, present your child with another, bigger box (perhaps a tissue box or a shoe box). Ask her how she can use what she's learned about the number of cubes in the small box to determine how many cubes might fit in the bigger box.

2–6

Boxes and More Boxes

Figure out how many of one kind of box will fit into another one. For example:

- How many toothpaste boxes fit in a laundry soap box?
- How many tissue boxes fit in the box the oranges came in?
- How many juice boxes fit in the Monopoly game box cover?

Use pencil or markers to draw in or mark how the smaller box fits in the bigger one. You probably won't have enough of the smaller boxes to completely fill the bigger one, which means that marking and keeping track—important mathematical skills in their own right—are essential.

Easier box questions involve one layer of boxes, such as the juice boxes in the Monopoly game box cover.

2–4

Harder box questions involve several layer boxes, with different shaped boxes (toothpaste boxes in a laundry soap box). Encourage older children to find how many smaller boxes would fit if you could cut them into pieces in order to use all of the space.

Cubes in a Cylinder

4-6

How many cubes will fit in an oatmeal box or other cylindrical box? The fit isn't so neat this time. Have your child begin by figuring out about how many cubes will fit in the cover of the box (or how many go in one layer). Here, it's important to think about partial pieces of cubes. One strategy is to draw the cover of the box on a piece of cardboard and trace around the cubes to see how many whole ones fit. Then start thinking about how the pieces fit. Once your child has decided about the number of cubes needed for one layer, use this information to figure out how many cubes fit in the entire box. See if she can generalize: "If you know how many cubes are in one layer, how does that help you figure out how many would be in a box twelve layers high? Twenty layers high?" Remember, using calculators is to be encouraged!

Making Your Own Empty Box

How can you make a box that fits a certain number of cubes?

K-2

Give younger children one layer of cubes, or perhaps just a row of cubes, along with construction paper, pencil, tape, and scissors. Ask them to make a box without a top that will hold all of the cubes just the way you've placed them on the table. Younger children may do this piece-meal, by making four different sides and a bottom. Encourage them to figure out how long each side of each piece should be. The focus should be on making a good fit.

2-4

Older children should be encouraged to make a simple, one-layer box *in one piece*. To do this, they'll have to think about how something flat can become something three-dimensional (in the lingo of mathematicians, it's a 2-D to 3-D transformation). Use plenty of paper and experiment with different folding techniques. See if you can make it so there's no "extra" paper when you fold.

4-6

Once one layer has been mastered, try making a box that has at least two layers or a box that has a cover. Again, try to make it all in one piece. If you're working with a set number of cubes (forty, for example), how many different rectangular-shaped boxes can you make?

NOTE

This activity is a good place to bring in common mathematical vocabulary in a natural way. Ask your child about the height, width, and length of the box she is making. Most of the boxes your child makes from cubes will be "rectangular solids," though the ones that have the same dimensions on all sides are cubes. Each side of the box is known as a "face."

gardening math

Whether you live in the city or country, gardening presents opportunities for kids to learn about measurement, space, and the rate at which plants grow. Gardening also is a great way to integrate mathematical and scientific concepts, such as how growth happens. Furthermore, gardening involves planning ahead by making maps and plots, which in turn involves making mathematical models that use scale. As many gardeners can attest, making these plans is a fine way to pass the time on cold winter evenings.

where's the math?

Just about every part of gardening involves mathematics. Gardening can include consumer math, studying and interpreting maps, using area, making measurements, finding volume, and charting growth. Activities in this section deal with three main mathematical ideas: (1) using benchmarks to make informal measurements, (2) making mathematical representations, and (3) studying growth.

Using benchmarks means using approximate measures, which is exactly what gardeners do to mark off distances. It's important for young children to get a concrete sense of the size of an inch, six inches, and a foot, and for older children to know about the size of various fractions of an inch. Research has shown that children need many, many experiences with "informal" measurement before they start using formal tools for measuring. One way of doing this is for children to find units that involve their own bodies—one of their feet may be about six inches, their handspan may be four inches—and use these units to mark off distances between seeds or plants.

Gardening also involves planning ahead, making maps, and using scale. Representations, in the form of plot plans drawn to scale, can help the gardener and budding mathematician determine how many plants will fit in a certain area. The garden plans children make are actually mathematical models, in which there are rules for figuring out how much space on graph paper is used to represent "actual" space. Making such translations, and generating mathematical rules to guide the translations, is a sophisticated and important idea in mathematics.

Studying and representing growth, or how things change, is an important part of algebra and calculus. Whenever children chart growth over time, they become more familiar with the idea of rates, including steadiness, speeding up, and slowing down. They begin to understand how the story of growth over time can be told with a representation and how these representations can communicate the mathematics of change to others.

Getting Set

You'll need all of your regular gardening tools, seeds, plants, and materials. In addition, paper and pencil—including graph paper—are necessary for making a garden plan. Finally, have on hand a variety of measuring tools, including string, ruler, and tape measure.

Plotting the Garden

K–2

Young children can get the idea of how to make a plan for the garden. Work with them to make a list of the flowers and vegetables that you want to have, then go out and examine your plot. How many plants of each kind will fit? Help your child estimate how big each plant will be when it is full-grown. Show how high it will be (height) and how much area it will take up. Use this information to modify your original list. Your child might want to write the final list, along with how many of each you'll have. Depending on your child's interest and skills, ask questions like the following: "How many more tomato plants will we have than cucumber plants?" "What's the smallest number of plants of one kind on our list? What's the largest?"

2–6

Walking your garden plot is also a good first step to take with older children, as it gives them a concrete sense of how much space is available. Older children should be encouraged to make pencil-and-paper plots, using whatever representations they think will work. Give them all the information about spacing of plants that they'll need and decide together what you might want to plant. Then have them draw the plot on graph paper. Right away, they'll encounter issues of scale: what shape should the plot be drawn, how big should it be, and what does that mean in terms of how the plants should be spaced? The idea of one foot being equivalent to one inch on paper is not immediately obvious to children. Graph paper helps with this, as children can establish how many "units" on the graph paper represent a certain distance. Of course, they'll have to measure the plot first. Once they've gotten the plot drawn, they'll need to use their graph paper and scale to figure out where everything should go.

NOTE

Some children love the precision of the planning process. You may need to remind them that things won't be so exact once you get outside!

Measuring Distance with Benchmarks

K–2

When planting seeds, help your child figure out the spacing of the seeds by establishing some personal "benchmarks." For example, tell your child that the distance between seeds should be about the same as the length of one of his feet. How many seeds will fit in the whole row? Your child can pace off and count his paces to figure it out. Similarly, some seeds need to be spaced one "hand span" apart, while others might need to go the length of a finger apart. This is a good opportunity to talk about measurement units, such as inches and feet.

2~4

Older children can begin figuring out their own personal benchmarks. When you see instructions for spacing seeds or plants, say something like this to your child: "The carrots need to be planted about two inches apart. About how far is that? What could you use to help you think about how far it is?" Children might choose something on their own bodies (e.g., the length of a finger), or perhaps they'll select something related to a gardening tool they're using (the length of a trowel blade, for example).

Measuring Depth with Benchmarks

This is similar to the previous activity, but you need some smaller benchmarks. Lettuce is often planted at 1/8" depth. How deep is that? Is your fingernail longer or shorter than that?

K~2

You might want to simply point out appropriate benchmarks to younger children and then have them use the benchmark as they go along planting.

K~4

Older children might want to find their own benchmarks by using a ruler to get a sense of the different distances. It's especially interesting for them to work with fractions of an inch, as it helps them discover the relationship between $\frac{1}{8}$, $\frac{1}{4}$, $\frac{1}{2}$, etc., and figure out for themselves which of these fractions is smaller and which is bigger.

How Much Fertilizer?

4~6

Dealing with area, volume, and proportion is a key part of gardening. Introduce children to the idea that you need a certain amount of fertilizer *per* unit of water or soil. This idea is easiest to introduce with liquid fertilizer, as you typically need a certain amount per gallon of water. Mixing in the right amount of fertilizer per unit of soil is a little harder. Here is a typical problem for older children: "The fertilizer label says we should use eight cups per hundred square feet of surface in our garden. How much fertilizer should we use?" There are many ways of solving this problem, and it's important to let your children work it through themselves. You might wonder aloud how many square feet are in your own garden and perhaps explain what a square foot is. Then, children can work it through by discussing possible strategies with parents or each other, making their own measurements, and determining area in their own way.

Family Project: Charting the Amaryllis

Some plants, like the amaryllis, grow quickly enough that it's interesting to keep a daily growth record. If you have an amaryllis or similar plant, put it out at the appropriate time and watch for signs of early growth. Tell your family that sometimes these plants grow very quickly, and you're eager to see how long it takes before it blooms. Everyone in your family can make and record predictions.

There are at least two things for you to measure and keep track of: how tall the plant is each day, and how much it grows each day. Discuss how these two things are related and decide what you'll measure. Get out some graph paper and figure out how to make a daily record. If your child already knows about graphing, she'll probably make a standard graph, but this isn't necessary at all! Encourage your child to invent her own way of recording, one that will show how much the plant grows from day to day or how tall it is at different times. Then, take the measurements each day. Family members can take turns at this, or one child can be responsible. Post the chart in a prominent place for everyone to see. Once you've got at least a week's worth of data, take a look at it. What do you notice? How fast does the plant seem to be growing? Is it growing faster or slower now than it was in the beginning, or is it growing at a steady rate? Based on what we've seen so far, how much do we expect it to grow next week?

great outdoors math

Hiking, biking, camping, canoeing, and fishing—all are great ways of spending time together as a family. There's a good deal of math to do when you're outdoors. Many of the activities below are best undertaken in local, state, or national parks, which contain a wealth of environmental as well as mathematical information, from 3-D maps to descriptions of natural phenomena to guided tours. Don't overlook the naturalist programs, either, as they are packed with scientific information that has a mathematical bent.

where's the math?

Measurement, along with working with the results of these measurements, is critical to many outdoor activities. Often the measurement is distance, and sometimes it is volume, depth, or height. Children are willing to take special care with these measurements, because they are immediate and important. Deciding whether you can hike the 1.2 mile trail before lunch has real implications, especially when you know you'll be hungry if you misjudge.

Measurement involves *direction-giving, pacing, map-making,* and *map-reading,* which are multifaceted mathematical skills. All of these skills involve spatial reasoning. For younger children, the task is often how to orient themselves and how to match directions with the intended outcome. For all children, outdoor activities are perfect for teaching map-reading, whether it's using a campground map to find your campsite, a topographical map of the lake to figure out depth, or trail maps to chart your course for the day.

Be aware that the impromptu math that happens during outdoor activities extends far beyond measurement. What math you choose to do depends on where you are and what you encounter in your travels. When you discover that 249 bald eagles were spotted in the state park this year—compared with only 17 a few years ago, it's only natural to wonder aloud, "How many more are there this year?" Children are especially engaged by dramatic environmental statistics and changes.

Getting Set

You will be making use of the material you collect on your travels. Never pass up a brochure that contains mathematical information about the place you're visiting. Most important of these are maps. In addition to maps of the place you are visiting, you'll need paper and markers for making your own maps and sets of directions.

Camping

With your child, identify some landmarks in the campground. Ask him or her to make a "pace map" showing where these things are. (Note: A pace

K–4

is a "regular-sized step.") On a large sheet of paper, mark the position of your campsite, then ask your child to find out and show on the map how far it is to the bathrooms, wood pile, office, trail head, etc. Somewhat older children will enjoy the same activity, but encourage them to describe and show turns, as well as direct distances. As an added challenge, have children read off their directions to you or their brother/sister and see where you get!

K–4

Ask children to help you determine whether your tent will fit in the spot that you've chosen. Using twigs (or chalk), have the child make a rectangle on the ground showing how the tent will fit in the place you've chosen. As you set up the tent, talk about the child's estimate and compare it to the actual amount of space covered by the tarp. This is a good opportunity to very naturally incorporate some mathematical language (width, length, area, bigger than, smaller than).

K–4

One of the special challenges of camping is bringing enough water to the campsite. In our everyday lives, we rarely think about how much water we need. This changes dramatically when you're camping, especially if you're backpacking.

Ask children to estimate how many buckets or cups of water you'll need for: (*a*) drinking, (*b*) washing dishes, (*c*) making food, and (*d*) cleanup. You may want to give your child his/her own bucket, special scoop, or large plastic cup for checking out his/her estimates.

4–6

When backpacking or doing day hikes, figure out about how much water you'll need per person and what this means in terms of the amount each person should carry. Many hiking experts recommend carrying at least 2 cups per person per hour. (More will be needed in hot weather or if the trip is especially strenuous.) How does this translate to the trip you've planned today? Given this amount, figure out how much the canteens or water bottles hold and how much each person will need to carry.

Maps and Distance

When you're in a campground or near a hiking/biking trail, look carefully at the maps that are available and take a copy of any map offered at the office.

K–2

Find out where we are now. Which way should we go to get to the parking lot, picnic area, lake, etc.? How far are they? Young children need experience linking the stated distance with the actual experience of walking or biking it. Help them discover how long it takes to cover a mile or a kilometer.

Some places have 3-D maps that give a very good sense of how flat or high or jagged the terrain is. Children are attracted to these maps, because they have much more concrete information than the usual flat map. If you encounter one of these, spend some time examining it. Once you've identified where you are now, ask your child questions like:

> Are we in a low spot or a high spot? How do you know?
> We're going to hike over here. What will our route be like? I know that first we'll be going down, but what happens here? Then what?
> If we want to go to the highest place in the park, where do we go?

We can go about ___ miles (kilometers) before lunch. What routes could we take? If we go out and back on this bike trail, how far will it be altogether? Given that most distances that can be reasonably hiked/biked by children will be shown in miles and tenths of miles, this is a great opportunity to add decimal values. (If children haven't encountered the notation before, explain that .4 is the same as $\frac{4}{10}$. If they haven't encountered fractions before, you may want to stick with whole numbers.)

Some maps do not show the distance of various trails. This is an excellent opportunity to work with the map's scale to determine distances. To help with this, break off a twig (or use a string) that represents a certain distance (e.g., $\frac{1}{2}$ mile, 1 kilometer). Have children follow the trail route on the map and estimate how far it is. Pay particular attention to working with segments of the trail that aren't straight lines.

Water Depth Measurements

You'll need a topographical map of the lake for this. Give children the basics about how to read the map (what the lines mean, how they show depth). Raise questions like the following to help children interpret the map:

> Where's the deepest part of the lake? The shallowest? Where would you expect to see the most weeds? Why? Where could you swim in this lake if you didn't want to be anywhere over your head?

2→6

Where are the steepest drop-offs in the lake? Are there any places that are not near shore where it's especially shallow?"

4→6

We know that ____ (kind of fish you're interested in) like to swim where it's between ___ and ___ feet deep. Where should we try fishing?

cooking and eating math

On a daily basis, the most predictable and regular opportunities for mathematical thinking are mealtime, snacktime, and cleanup time. There's a range of math you can do during these times, involving activities such as measurement, finding fractions, dividing, and comparing. You also need to find containers for your leftovers almost every day, which provides an opportunity for children to explore measurement of volume (we hope without spilling too much!).

where's the math?

Many of these activities are about dividing. Sometimes, food comes in pieces and division involves counting and distributing these things into "fair shares." Other times, food comes in pans in the shapes of squares, rectangles, and circles—and the job is to figure out how to divide *area*. Both kinds of division are mathematically important, and both can lead into thinking about fractions of a whole (e.g., dividing a whole bag of popcorn, a whole pan of meatloaf).

Another mathematical skill, emphasized particularly in the "leftovers" activities, involves thinking about volume and how it is measured. Most cooks have an intuitive sense of how much food will fit in different-sized containers: this intuition is built on an understanding of conservation of volume, which Piaget studied with elementary school children. Children gradually learn that you have to consider all aspects of a three-dimensional shape—its height, length, and width—in order to figure out which containers have the same volume. Figuring out which containers to use for leftovers is a natural way to help children develop these skills.

The new nutritional labels can help your child with a third area of mathematics: number sense. It is important for children to understand that foods differ in terms of their nutritional value and that there are quantitative ways of identifying and comparing nutritional value. Finding the highest and lowest number of fat grams in the boxes of food in your cupboard allows children to place numbers on a continuum and get a sense of range and variation. Comparing the fat content of different crackers, cereals, or yogurts gives children an idea of the relationship between quantities and at the same time may even help them make better decisions as a consumer.

Getting Set

For these activities, you need the things that are already in your kitchen. It helps to have measuring cups and spoons that are clearly marked, as well as a variety of containers for leftovers. If you have older children, bring out all those odd-shaped cooking pans and containers you have stored in the basement. If you have a postage scale or food scale, you can use it to establish what a "gram" is before beginning the nutritional labeling activities.

Dividing Pans of Food

How many people are here? How big is the pan of brownies? How many pieces do we need to divide it into? These are questions that kids of all ages care about. The difficulty of the problems depends on the size of the group you are cooking for, as well as the shape of the container that you are using. Even very young children can work with dividing a small square cake into four equal-sized pieces. Older children can handle larger numbers and the idea that pieces don't have to look identical in order to be the same size.

Bring out the pan of lasagna. We have to divide this into twelve pieces about the same size. So how should we cut it? Where should we make the cut marks?

K-4

Use pans that are shaped in circles, squares, and rectangles—and bring out those odd-shaped Jell-O molds, too. Trace the pan on a piece of cardboard or heavy paper and have kids practice (with pencil) making lines to show the different ways you could cut the food to make fair-sized pieces. Do all the pieces need to look the same? Challenge your child to make pieces that are the same in area but look different. Someone might get a long triangular brownie, someone else a square—but your child should try to prove that they have the same area.

2-6

Children can cut out the cardboard pieces when they have a plan and overlay them on each other to check out whether they are equal in area. Finally, they can help you place the cuts, or make the cuts themselves if they're old enough.

Do We Have Enough?

Have your child count the rolls, fruit, cookies, or other "pieces" of food you want to distribute for meals or snacks. Is there enough for everyone? How many can each person have if we want to use all of it?

K-2

A variation of this activity is to do a "count" of how many rolls or pieces of chicken, etc., each person will eat. Ask the child to figure out, based on the information s/he's collected, whether there will be enough to go around.

2-4

When you're down to that last fraction of a container of milk or juice, ask the kids to figure out how many it can serve. This works well for syrup on pancakes, too—how much longer will it last? Will we need more before we go shopping on Saturday? If three people have pancakes each time, how many pancake breakfasts can we have? Try this with large as well as small quantities.

Will It fit?

Before you get to the problem of whether anyone will eat leftovers, you face the problem of storage. The pot of soup has dwindled, and you want to store the leftovers in a smaller container. Which size is best? Have your child puzzle through these leftover storage decisions with you. You might start a conversation this way:

> The soup pot is less than half full now, and it won't fit in the refrigerator. I'm wondering if you can choose a smaller container for it. We have these three containers we could put it in. Which do you think will fit it best?

Depending on the age of the child, bring out issues like this in the conversation:

- Look at all dimensions. A storage container may be both shorter and narrower than the original. Is it tall enough to hold the leftovers? How do you know?
- Are there built-in measures on the container? If so, use them to estimate: "This container says it holds two quarts, which is eight of these cups. Do you think we have that much in the pan?"
- When doing an estimate with leftovers, the consequences of overestimating aren't the same as those of underestimating! You must make sure you have enough space in the leftover container, so your estimate might be more conservative than usual.

A simple activity that is a favorite in our family involves figuring out how to use cookie cutters most efficiently. How can you fit the shapes together so that you have the most cookies and the least amount of dough left over? (You might want to explain that dough gets tougher each time you roll it out, so it's important to get the most out of each time you roll.) Roll out separate pieces of dough for each child who's working on the project and encourage them to think about how the pieces might fit *before* they actually cut them. Kids of different ages learn a lot from watching each other and listening to each other's strategies.

Nutrition Scavenger Hunt

Remember sitting at the breakfast table and reading the backs of the cereal boxes? These days, there are numbers on the back of nearly every box, bag, or can of food in your house. You can learn how many calories, how much sodium and protein, and how much fat is in every serving of everything you eat. Use any packaged foods for these activities.

Choose a cupboard and ask your child to examine the labels and find the item with the most and the fewest grams of fat.

Make a list of your favorite snack foods. Find the grams of fat in each of these. Which are the healthier snacks?

Have the kids sort food from a cupboard into foods that "go together." For example, categories might be salty snacks, dessert foods, main dish foods. Your child might even choose to make a category like "foods I don't like." Make a list of each food in each category and how much fat it contains. Which category had items with the most fat? Which category had items with the least fat? What surprises were there?

Reducing the Fat

How many grams' worth of butter do you put on your bread or toast? How much would you save if you used jam instead?

Compare the fat content of *low-fat* and *regular* versions of the same dairy food (e.g., milk, yogurt, margarine, ice cream, cream cheese). How many grams of fat do you eliminate each time you choose the low-fat version? Make a list to show how much you'd save for each of these items.

School math and beyond

four

What to Look for at School

Up till now, the focus of this book has been on what parents can do directly to help their children with mathematics. This work is difficult but immediately gratifying. It is at least as challenging to try to figure out how we can get and support high quality mathematics learning at school. The challenges include knowing what to look for in a math class and knowing how to support a good math program when you see it.

A Tale of Two Classrooms

Parents often ask, "What should I be looking for in a good math classroom? How will I know if the teacher is doing a good job and what can I do to support her?" It would be handy to have a basic checklist to use in evaluating mathematical activity in the classroom, but it's not that easy. What you are looking for is a classroom in which children's skills in constructing mathematics for themselves are valued and emphasized. See if you can tell the difference between the role of the students, as well as that of the teacher, in these two classrooms.

Mr. Hale's Class

Mr. Hale's third graders are embarking on a new unit: subtraction involving three-digit numbers, with borrowing. Mr. Hale begins with a review of the steps of borrowing. He reminds children how to borrow a 10, and demonstrates the appropriate crossing-out marks on the board. Then he presents the problem, 328 − 79, and shows how the borrowing procedure can be extended to bigger numbers. Throughout this talk, he asks for students to help him solve the problems, and there are a few students who explain the correct procedures. After checking to see if there are any questions, Mr. Hale asks the children to work individually on a set of twenty problems from the textbook, while he goes around the class to observe. Later, he will review the procedures with the children, model the proper procedures when students are having problems, and assign homework so that children can practice.

While Mr. Hale observes his students working, he sees a variety of borrowing. Some are correct, while others are systematic or ingenious but don't yield the correct answer. For example, Jamie "borrows" in every problem, whether he needs to or not. Mr. Hale reminds Jamie that borrowing is only necessary when the top number is smaller than the bottom number. Jamie does the next problem correctly while Mr. Hale watches.

Another student, Sasha, is working on this problem:

Mr. Hale sees that Sasha is getting mixed up in her crossing-out steps. Mr. Hale corrects her procedure and also reminds her that a good way of checking her answer is to add up the bottom two numbers and see if she gets the top number. Sasha is surprised that her answer has not worked but tries to do the problem again, using what Mr. Hale has taught her.

As the children work, they occasionally share their answers with each other. "What did you get?" is a common question. When there are disagreements about the answer, children frequently change their answers so that they conform with the answers of the kids who are "good" at math.

Ms. Russell's Class

Ms. Russell's third graders are working on a unit on combining and comparing (from the TERC curriculum, "Investigations in Number, Data, and Space"). Yesterday, Ms. Russell asked each child to find out how old his/her oldest living relative is. Today, she begins class by writing "128 years old" on the board. She asks the class if anyone has a relative that old and then explains that 128 is the record age that anyone has ever lived. From the *Guinness Book of Records*, she reads the children a description of the record-holder, which prompts lots of questions about longevity. Ms. Russell reminds the children that they and their partners will be working with the data they brought in from home to address this question:

"How much longer would your oldest relative need to live in order to tie the record?"

Ms. Russell reminds the children that while solving this problem, they should use any tools in the classroom that might help them, including calculators, cubes, buttons, and other counters. She also reminds them to keep track of their work and to write a couple of sentences telling how they figured out the problem. Children get settled in pairs, choose their materials, and begin to work.

Danny and Carlos have started with Carlos's 88-year-old grandfather. Carlos is excited by this number, because he figures it should be easy to get from 88 to 128 by counting tens. Together, the boys count 88–98–108–118–128. As they do so, Danny raises one finger for each ten. They know they have 40, because it's four tens. Ms. Russell encourages them to write down the strategy they used and to prove that it works in another way. They decide to use the calculator to prove it.

Nick and Jenny are working with buttons. Nick's great-aunt is 92. They've decided to put one button out for each birthday that Nick's great-aunt will have to have until she reaches 128. The children carefully count 93, 94, 95, 96, etc., as they lay out a button for each number.

When the pairs of children have finished, class members discuss a few of the comparisons and share their strategies. Many children comment that they have different strategies than the ones their classmates used. Ms. Russell assigns a homework problem: she asks students to figure out how much longer *they* would have to live to tie the record. "Can I figure it out for my mom and dad, too?" asks Shanti. Ms. Russell encourages them to make whatever comparisons they want to.

You are probably quite familiar with classrooms like Mr. Hale's. It is clear what Mr. Hale's starting point is, as he is building on a procedure that children already know. His presentation style is easy to follow, and children know what to expect. Mr. Hale introduces a problem, demonstrates how it should be solved, assigns individual "seat work," checks in with the class, then assigns homework that involves children in practicing the skill they have just learned. Students who listen carefully and follow Mr. Hale's procedures may be able to perform the work, but they may not understand what they are doing. In classes like these, students don't address the question: "Does my answer make sense?" Mr. Hale's job, as he sees it, is to intervene with students who are making errors and get them on the right track before misconceptions become ingrained.

Classrooms like Ms. Russell's, while not the norm, are becoming more common. Ms. Russell poses a problem for students without giving them techniques for solving it. She expects that they will use their mathematical understanding to invent their own strategies for solving a problem. She also knows that children will solve the problem using strategies that make sense to them individually. Ms. Russell expects this diversity and encourages it by providing a range of materials for students to work with. Another key ingredient of Ms. Russell's classroom is the cooperative element to solving problems. Children learn from each other, share their ideas for approaching problems, and communicate through writing, drawing, and explaining. Logical explanations are of utmost importance.

You may not have noticed, but the students in both classes were working on the same kinds of three-digit subtraction problems. Yet, the focus of these classes is entirely different. Mr. Hale focuses on how borrowing is done, with the expectation that students will master this procedure. By contrast, Ms. Russell is purposely not teaching her third graders the borrowing procedure. She expects them to develop ways of solving the problem based on their knowledge of numbers and their composition. Ways of doing the problem may well differ from individual to individual. The critical difference between these teachers is in their expectations for children: do children generate sound mathematical strategies on their own or do they learn to follow a strategy presented by the teacher? Here are the main differences between these two classrooms:

Mr. Hale's Class	Ms. Russell's Class
Children are taught a standard procedure for subtracting.	Children use their own strategies for comparing, including adding on by ones or tens.
The teacher's role is to present information and monitor children's progress in assimilating this information.	The teacher's role is to identify how children can extend their own understanding of the math.
Children work with pencil and paper.	Children work with a variety of tools, including the calculator.
Children do problems from a textbook in which the operation is clear.	Children do problems in which the "procedure" is not predefined.
Homework is to practice the procedure.	Homework is to provide more opportunities to consolidate strategies, gather data, think about and report on findings.
Children work individually, and each is expected to master the procedure.	Children learn from each other as well as the teacher.
The outline for the class session is clear, systematic, and predetermined.	The class session is fluid and depends on children's progress.
Getting the right answer, along with the correct procedure, is emphasized.	Explaining your strategy and making mathematical sense is valued.

There is another difference worth mentioning between these classrooms. Mr. Hale rarely is questioned by parents concerning the approach he is taking to math. His approach is familiar to parents, and he gets along well with students and encourages them to be productive. Ms. Russell, on the other hand, receives both more questions and more complaints from parents. She often feels as if she is swimming upstream in her attempt to have children develop their own mathematical understanding. Her perception is that she gets little support from parents.

The Ingredients of a Good Math Program

If you are convinced that children need to learn to think, understand, and behave mathematically, you should be looking for classrooms like Ms. Russell's. Your child's teacher should know that mathematics is more than a collection of facts and believe that mathematical understanding depends on having children construct it for themselves. This is the most important thing to look for. But beyond this, there are some other ingredients to effective school mathematics programs. While no school can perfectly implement a math program across the board, there are guidelines against which a math program should be assessed.

Commitment to NCTM Standards

The school should express and *enact* a commitment to the math standards developed by the National Council of Teachers of Mathematics (NCTM). At the very least, the administrators and teachers at your child's school should be acquainted with the reform movement in mathematics. Unfortunately, knowing about this and doing something about it are two different things. Many textbook publishers have tried to reform themselves by making surface changes, and so have many schools. However, a deeper commitment to reform is usually accompanied by changes in behavior, not just changes in rhetoric. Good indicators that a school is committed to real change include the following:

- The district is undertaking a review of textbooks and curriculum to see if these are optimal in terms of promoting mathematical understanding.
- Funds are being devoted to teachers' ongoing professional development.
- Support and encouragement are given to teachers who are using new curricula or curricula they have developed on their own.
- The school makes efforts to communicate with families about how and why mathematics education is changing.
- The school is devoting less money to textbooks and workbooks and more money to purchasing "math manipulatives"

(calculators, counters, blocks, geometric shapes, materials that show the base-10 system).
- The school is experimenting with new ways to evaluate and report on students' progress in math.

What you should look for is a real commitment to change, accompanied by at least some action steps that indicate the commitment is sincere.

Teachers Who Value Students' Strategies

Do most teachers at the school value children's ability to do mathematics? Many teachers know how to help children become real writers, writers who create their own stories (and use their own idiosyncratic spelling when their vocabulary outpaces their spelling). The same teachers have a harder time thinking of children as real mathematicians, who create their own hypotheses, theorems, and strategies. It is a good sign if your child's teacher engages in a process approach to writing or has established a whole language classroom. This indicates that at least with respect to reading and writing, the teacher values each child's ability to make sense of language. Teachers like these may well be able to link what they are doing in language arts with what they ought to be doing in math. Parents can help teachers make this link by providing support and encouragement.

Evidence of Meaningful Math

In the classroom, there should be evidence that children are doing meaningful math, that they are communicating mathematical ideas to each other, and that they have the tools they need to do mathematical investigations. Good indicators are:

- The classroom has a variety of manipulatives—blocks, counters, cubes, rods, string, buttons, and calculators—and they are placed within easy reach of children. Manipulatives that are on high shelves or in the closet do no good.
- Children's work is posted, and it is not of the cookie-cutter variety. Identical worksheets are a sign that everyone is expected to do the same procedures. Look for children's writing and drawing about the way they solved problems. Look for 3-D models as well.
- There should be evidence that bigger mathematical projects are going on. This may come in the form of charts or graphs about data collection or other mathematical projects. There could also be evidence that a special mathematics activity, such as weaving, drawing patterns, or building marble chutes, is being undertaken.
- Mathematical questions are present in the classroom for children to consider. These might be as simple as "How many

apples did we pick on our field trip?" Children are invited to address these problems. Sometimes questions like this become a systematic part of the classroom and are labeled "problem of the day" or "problem of the week."

- The mathematical work of each child is collected. Students may have a math folder or portfolio, or may keep math journals. This archive of children's work should consist mainly of their mathematical problem solving, reflecting, and activity (routine worksheets don't count for much).

The Acceptance of Computers as Tools

If the math program involves computers, they should be used as tools or to explore real mathematics and not for drill and practice. While computers are not an essential component of mathematics programs at the elementary school level, they can be very powerful learning tools if good software is selected. When teachers or administrators boast about the number of computers or ratio of students to computers in their schools, they're missing the point. Ask school personnel how computers are being used in math. The software that children use should encourage mathematical understanding. For example, Logo is a classic and excellent tool that involves children in mapping, programming, geometry, and mathematical constructions. Since the inception of Logo, there have been many interesting extensions, especially ones like Lego-Logo in which children create and program their own toys, vehicles, gears, and amusement parks.

Besides the major tools like Logo, look for classroom games that involve pattern-finding, logic, geometry, and number sense. Examples of good software are discussed in the Resources chapter. Look also for the use of "tool" software such as data bases and spreadsheets. These tools allow students to work with data and numbers and to see the effects of changes that they make.

Unfortunately, there are many trivial and even harmful computer applications that are quite popular in math classes. If teachers talk about computers as motivational tools or suggest that computers are used to "reinforce concepts," it could be a sign that the machines are being used as electronic workbooks. Electronic workbooks are no better than any other kind. They give children the message that math is about knowing the right answer. With this software, the quicker you have memorized information at your fingertips, the more points and rewards you get. This is not the message we should be giving children about mathematics.

Some Danger Signs

As you evaluate the math program in your child's school, there are some signals that should alert you to the fact that memorization and procedures are being emphasized too much. If you notice any of the following, talk to your child's teacher about the goals of the math curriculum.

- *Regular timed tests on "math facts."* Students ought to learn to be fluent with math facts, but an emphasis on speed is a sign that procedures are being memorized more than math is being understood.
- *Homework consisting of dozens of similar computational problems.* Homework tells you what is valued by the teacher. If it looks as if children are being asked to memorize a procedure and apply it over and over again, find out whether this is happening in math class as well as on homework.
- *A teacher who makes calculators (or counting on fingers) off-limits.* Calculators ought to be available to students most or all of the time in math class and for homework. Similarly, children ought to be encouraged to use their fingers, toes, or anything else that is convenient to solve problems that are difficult for them.
- *A constant emphasis on arithmetic.* The work that your child brings home, as well as that done in class, ought to reflect a balanced mathematical diet. This means they should do work with geometric patterns, logic, data, and estimation, as well as with numbers.
- *Math competitions that stress quick calculation rather than careful, reflective problem solving.* Children get the wrong idea about math if competitions like these are a major part of the program.

Supporting Effective Math Programs

What if your child is not in a classroom or school that promotes mathematical power? There are many avenues for helping a school develop a better mathematics program. First, talk to your child's teacher about this book and what you are doing at home to promote mathematical thinking. Ask if there are ways you can help your child and be a more active participant in math homework. If parent volunteers are welcome in the classroom, offer to come in and read the children a book that is rich in mathematics. On a schoolwide level, join or start a parent group on mathematics to acquaint yourselves with what's happening in the field and develop a presence for reforming mathematics in your school. Parent groups can be very effective and powerful advocates for change.

If your children are lucky enough to attend a school where good things are already happening in math, don't take it for granted! Talk with your children's teachers or the principal about how you can help support the mathematics program. Offer to help out with a parent math night, or better still, talk with other parents about the strengths you see in the math program. Show your appreciation. Sign up to participate on the math curriculum committee and help review the "alternative" mathematics curricula that are being considered for adoption. Generate financial support for teachers who wish to attend workshops and conferences that will help them develop better approaches to teaching. And above all, offer moral support to teachers who are engaged in the very difficult process of changing the ways that mathematics is taught.

For teachers, one of the critical ingredients in promoting change is parental support. At math workshops, we frequently hear teachers say, "I could never change my math program that way. The parents would never stand for it." Make it known that you are a parent who will not only welcome change, but help educate others about how mathematics education needs to be transformed. Your support may well make a critical difference in a teacher's willingness to risk new approaches to teaching and learning math.

five

That's a Good Question

As parents, we have little to draw on from our own mathematical experiences that helps us address the issues that arise with our children. That means you can anticipate having many questions as you get involved in your child's mathematical life. Each of the following could be its own chapter in this book and deserves a more thorough answer than space allows. Perhaps the best answer to any of these questions is this: find others who share your concern—other parents, teachers, the school principal—and talk more about it. Your concerns are important and need to be heard by those who are involved in your child's education.

My second grader seems good at math problem solving and seems to enjoy it. But even though he can figure out addition and subtraction problems, he hasn't memorized the facts. Should I be worried?

Not at all. You are very fortunate to have a child who can think through mathematical problems. If he can quickly figure out how much 9 + 5 is by using more familiar situations (10 + 5 = 15), then he is in fine shape. Your goal should be for him to become a fluent, capable problem-solver, not a brainless human calculator. Make sure he gets a lot of experience with everyday situations that involve calculation, and he'll begin to remember addition/subtraction "facts" that commonly come up. Even if he doesn't memorize them all, it's not critical that he do so. If he has tests at school, he can always use his basic understanding of how numbers fit together to derive what he needs to solve a given problem. If his teacher is using timed tests, try to gently dissuade her from this practice, perhaps by pointing out that the National Council of Teachers of Mathematics discourages rote memorization of facts.

There are a few things to be wary of. Commercially available tutoring programs in math often emphasize the speedy memorization of facts.

Enrolling your child in one of these would probably be a mistake, as it would not build on his strengths as a problem-solver and would constrict his view of what mathematics is. The same holds true for flash cards and software that emphasize speed. The drawback with these is that they place speed and memorization on a pedestal, when these are not the crucial mathematical skills your child needs. Better activities focus on mental math strategies (e.g., Monopoly and the card game 21). And while some folks might advise you to keep calculators away from your son, I'd recommend exactly the opposite: give him his own calculator for his birthday and encourage him to explore what it does. By playing with number patterns on the calculator, your child will gain more familiarity with them.

My daughter is in the fifth grade and seems to be losing interest in math. What can I do?

You are not alone. Fifth and sixth grade girls, though still as adept as boys in their mathematical skills, often begin to lose interest in this subject and feel that they are "not good at" math. Looking around them, they see that boys are more engaged in math. Boys are usually the first to raise their hands in math class, and teachers may call on boys more than they call on girls. If your daughter is experiencing a drop in mathematical interest or confidence, or even if she is simply noticing the gender differences that are emerging in her classroom, it is important that you take action. Here are some steps you might consider:

- First, talk to her teacher, let her know what is happening, and find out what is going on in school. Are boys dominating discussions, or is your daughter feeling that she isn't fast enough to get a chance to share her mathematical ideas? Do some thinking with the teacher, and let her know that you expect her to do everything she can to get the girls involved.
- Talk with your daughter about the sexist attitudes she may encounter and figure out some ways of coping with these unfair attitudes. She needs to know that boys and girls are equally capable of doing math. Don't be afraid to point out that most jobs that involve mathematics are higher paying than those that do not.
- If you are a mother, it is especially important that you do math with your daughter. Don't leave it to dad. She needs to see that you value math, think it is important, and want to do it with her. If you do math at work, or if there are women colleagues whose jobs involve mathematics, make sure to give your daughter the opportunity to visit.
- Have high expectations. Let your daughter know that you expect her to do well in all of her schoolwork, including math.
- Encourage your daughter to participate in after-school activities

that involve math. Science museums and children's museums are good places to start. Some even have "girls' only" programs in math and science, and these have been shown to be extremely effective in giving girls some breathing room and time to explore without feeling pressured. Some Girl Scout groups are also involved in special math and science projects.

I have a third-grade boy who sees a resource teacher, and she told me that children like mine need to learn math in small, sequential steps. Is she right?

Your child, like all others, will learn math best if he makes sense of it his own way. There is no research evidence to support the contention that children with learning disabilities need to have math organized in a more detailed way or broken down into small component parts. Try to work with the specialist to figure out your child's learning strengths. Is he a good visual learner? If so, perhaps he'll learn about multiplication more effectively by thinking about "arrays"—the way that candy or soda pop or eggs are organized in a box. He might invent and experiment with many different arrays on his own. Whatever he does mathematically should build on his learning strengths, rather than focus on his weaknesses.

Another important point to keep in mind is that children do not need to master one skill (e.g., memorization of addition facts to the number 20) before they can go on to the next level of mathematical skill. Contrary to what we have been led to believe, mathematics learning is not "ladder-like." Many students, for example, find multiplication much easier than certain kinds of subtraction. Students in resource rooms, like all students, should have many opportunities to explore different forms of mathematics and to go beyond arithmetic. While it may be useful to focus their energies for a while on one particular area, if they are making little headway it is time to try something else. Some children in special education classes end up spending many frustrating months, even years, trying to memorize procedures and facts. They are held back to focus on mathematics they have trouble with and are prevented from learning mathematics that would be exciting and challenging. This is a waste of time and truly gets in the way of your child's learning significant mathematics.

It's important for your child to have an opportunity to work with peers who have a wide range of strategies for solving mathematical problems. He may see that Jamie has an interesting way of doing fair share problems that is different than his own, and he might then experiment with Jamie's method. He may become fascinated with Elena's way of making halves and ask her to explain what she is doing. He needs many opportunities to do this kind of exploring and sharing within his regular classroom, as well as in the resource room.

My child seems to be especially good at math. She thinks about it constantly and solves some problems more quickly than I do. What can I do to help her at home—and what kind of program should she be in at school?

It's great to have an avid mathematician in the house. Some parents panic at the thought, but you shouldn't. Eventually, most of our children will be better mathematicians than we are, especially if we do our jobs right! It's reassuring to remember that there are many areas in which children are more skilled than their parents: many ten-year-old kids are much better soccer players than their parents, but parents can still help them learn. How? Here are some suggestions:

- Ask your child to explain how she is thinking about a problem. She should be able to explain it in a way that makes sense to you. This helps her think flexibly and helps you understand more mathematics.
- Encourage *metacognitive* skills (the ability to think about how one is learning). Ask your child to tell you how her thinking about one problem helped her to solve another, whether she has a certain way of doing a certain kind of problem, etc.
- Show a genuine interest and pleasure in her learning. If your child makes a mathematical discovery, be delighted for her— whether you understand the discovery or not.

With respect to school programs, some experts would recommend an enriched or gifted program for a child like yours, while others would suggest keeping your child in the regular classroom. There are difficult trade-offs involved, and these are discussed in detail in the books recommended in Chapter 6. If you do place your child in a special program, make sure it is one that has real mathematical depth and is not simply an accelerated program that emphasizes whizzing through mathematical material at breakneck speed. A good program, on the other hand, may move even more *slowly* than a regular program, because it gives articulate children an opportunity to challenge and extend each other's strategies.

A crucial ingredient to any child's mathematical development is the teacher. A good teacher can support and guide children who are at varying levels of mathematical sophistication. She knows her task is to understand how a child is thinking and to extend that thinking through the problems she poses. This can be done well in a "regular" classroom, and educational experts are encouraging this kind of teaching for all children. Of course, it is not a reality in all classrooms. If you have input into a placement decision, observe carefully in the classrooms in question (using the guidelines in Chapter 4) and figure out how the teachers support real mathematical thinking.

How am I supposed to know how my child is doing in math? What do the test scores tell me? What does a grade tell me?

Standardized test scores tell you very little about how well your child understands math. It is dangerous to put much stock in these scores because of their limitations. In fact, mathematics educators are now recommending that standardized tests be eliminated over the next few years. These tests will be replaced by more authentic mathematical tasks, such as those already being developed by the New Standards Project (see Chapter 6). These new tasks demand good problem-solving skills, the ability to see a problem from more than one perspective, the ability to think flexibly, and an understanding of various areas of mathematics that go beyond arithmetic. Once these new assessments are in place, parents will have a better indicator of how their children are doing mathematically.

In the meantime, you can probably glean much more information about your child's mathematical skills by examining her work, talking with the teacher, and observing in the classroom. If you've been working with your child, you know a good deal about how she thinks. You may know that she is good at generating number patterns, likes thinking about the characteristics of numbers, solves fraction problems by thinking about area, and likes to build things that are highly symmetrical. But you're still asking, "Yes, but how is she *doing* in math?" To get a sense of that, turn to your child's classroom. Look at all of the student work posted on the bulletin boards to get a sense of where your child's skills fit in. Do your child's strategies work as well (or better) than those exhibited by the other children? If it's okay with the teacher, attend a math lesson or two and listen carefully to how children are solving problems. Does your child contribute to mathematical discussions? Are his contributions interesting and valued? These are all questions that you can and should bring up at parent/teacher conferences as well.

Grades, like tests, seldom tell you much about mathematical understanding. In order to make sense of grades, you need to know what the teacher values and how she has graded. In some classrooms, a high grade may mean that a child is a good memorizer but say nothing about how she thinks mathematically. Grades can serve as an indicator of effort or of how well-behaved the child is in the classroom, so you can't necessarily use them as a gauge of mathematical understanding. Talking to the teacher will help you understand a child's grade. If it is possible, ask the teacher to show you some of your child's work and indicate what criteria she uses as she is grading. In an increasing number of classrooms, teachers collect mathematical portfolios for each child. If your child is in such a class, it's a good sign. It provides a starting place for parents to learn how their child is progressing.

I *understand that children need to learn to understand math deeply. But what about their future? How will they cope with a more traditional math class in high school or in college when they have not been steeped in math procedures and facts?*

Deep down, a main worry is whether our children will be truly prepared. How will they cope with the real world of trigonometry courses? And how will they ever make it through college calculus if they aren't good at memorizing procedures?

This question is based on the assumption that mathematics instruction in high school and college has not changed and will not change. But this may be a faulty assumption. Increasingly, college professors are concerned that their students are ill-prepared. What concerns them most is that students are not able to think but instead merely regurgitate formulas. These professors would much prefer to have a student who knows how to think mathematically but doesn't recognize all of the procedures than one who can memorize procedures but doesn't know or care how to solve challenging mathematical problems. After all, professors themselves go far beneath the surface of mathematics, and they value this characteristic in their students.

There are significant, large-scale reform efforts underway (many of which are sponsored by the National Science Foundation) to change how high school and college mathematics are taught. Your children may encounter a very different high school program than the one we knew—perhaps a program that integrates geometry, algebra, trigonometry, and calculus. (See the description of the Integrated Math Program in Chapter 6.) Textbooks are being abandoned by many high school math instructors in favor of curricula that stress flexible and in-depth mathematical thinking. Even college mathematics courses are being changed significantly, with more than 40 percent of the calculus courses in the country now emphasizing a more conceptual approach. Students are asked to deal with complex problems. Will your child be prepared to deal with these more sophisticated problems? She won't if she's had a steady diet of drill and practice mathematics. Learning how to think mathematically requires experience, and the more experience you can give your child, the better prepared she'll be for the future.

But face it. Change is slow to come, and most children will experience mindless mathematics courses—and some of these courses will matter in terms of college admissions or decisions about placement. Ask yourself this. Will a child who is a strong, flexible mathematician really not do as well in these classes as a child whose strength is memorizing procedures? I'm willing to put my money on the child who has solid thinking and problem-solving skills. Like most parents, I've struggled with the preparation-for-real-life issue. When my daughter transferred from a school that emphasized mathematical problem solving to a school in which children covered textbook arithmetic problems and memorized procedures, it took her two months or so to catch on to the rules. And though she was critical of and disinterested in the new program, she did fine as soon as she knew what was expected. Furthermore, she continued to be an avid math problem-solver at home. While we could have prepared Erica by giving her workbooks for a few years before she encountered traditional math, I am glad we did not. A teacher and colleague of mine, Karen Economopoulos, puts it simply: "The best preparation for a bad experience is a good experience." Now there's an axiom to live by!

Six

What Next?

This book has barely skimmed the surface of an educational area in which a vast amount of important new research, curriculum development, and school reform is taking place. The mathematics reform movement is affecting educators at all levels, but it has not explained itself well to parents. However, it is leaving a trail of interesting and accessible policy statements and materials that are easy for parents to find and read. If you want to know more about the national reforms—and why these are so important to your child's future—read some of the books on the list that follows. If your school has not yet done much with mathematics reform, share these resources with your child's principal or teacher and get your parent/teacher organization involved in sponsoring a "math night." The materials listed below will help you get started. Finally, there are hundreds of mathematics materials and resources targeted to teachers that are also very well-suited to parent-child mathematics learning. I have recommended some of my own favorite math materials, and I guarantee that you will have as much fun as your child does in using them to explore mathematics.

Workshops and Awareness Activities for Parents

Family Math

This noteworthy program gives math education at home a real boost. Family Math is both a workshop series for families and the title of the group's book of exciting, easy-to-implement math activities. The premise of the program is that families need to do math together and that they may need a little support from each other in getting started. The Family Math workshops are often led by teams of parents and teachers. Sometimes the programs are sponsored by science museums or by community agencies. If you are interested, ask your child's principal where a Family

Math (or Family Science) workshop is being offered. If there are no offerings in your community, the book provides advice on how to start one yourself.

To order the book, send a check for $17 to U.C. Regents at this address:

Family Math
The Lawrence Hall of Science
University of California
Berkeley, CA 94720

Math Matters: Kids Are Counting on You

This informational packet, published by the PTA, includes a videotape, posters, home math suggestions, and materials to help organize parent meetings about math education. It is particularly useful for those who want to get other parents interested in the directions that the math reform movement is taking. It includes specific suggestions for what a PTA (or other parent group) can do over a year's period to strengthen home-school math connections.

Math Matters is available from:

The National PTA
700 North Rush Street
Chicago, IL 60611-2571
(312) 787-0977

Mathematics: What Are You Teaching My Child?

Designed by Marilyn Burns, a prominent and creative math educator, this video provides engaging, thoughtful vignettes and dialogues concerning why mathematics education must change. It demarcates the great contrast between mathematics classrooms as parents experienced them (complete with black and white photos of anxious children doing problems on the board) and today's math classrooms, where the emphasis is on thinking and constructing mathematics. The tape also shows the variety of mathematics that is needed on the job by different kinds of workers and demonstrates why schools must go beyond arithmetic if they are to do a good job of preparing students for the future. The tape is available from the Cuisenaire Company (see address and phone under Resources for Parents).

Good Math Books and Magazines

Bibliographies and Teaching Resources

There are hundreds of excellent mathematically based books for children. In recent years, a plethora of picture books with mathematical themes has been coming onto the market. In fact, there are almost a dozen resources that describe these picture books and tell how to use them to promote children's thinking. Some of the best of these resources are the following:

Burns, Marilyn. 1992. *Math and Literature K-3*. White Plains, NY: Math Solutions Publications.

While this book is primarily for Kindergarten through third-grade classroom teachers, just read between the lines, and you'll find many good ideas about how to "talk mathematics" with your child as a natural part of story-reading. The activities and discussions are based upon ten well-known children's stories. These activities are also great for encouraging your children to write as a way of explaining their mathematical ideas.

Griffiths, R., and M. Clyne. 1991. *Books You Can Count On: Linking Mathematics and Literature*. Portsmouth, NH: Heinemann.

The easy-to-follow format of this resource includes charts showing the mathematical focus of each book, its appropriateness for children of various grade levels (most are for grades Kindergarten through fourth grade), and a synopsis of each book. The authors recommend several activities to do in conjunction with the stories— activities which include calculation, writing stories and poetry, and projects such as using catalogs to decide how to spend a certain amount of money. Most all of the activities in the book are equally appropriate for use at home and at school.

Sheffield, Stephanie. 1995. *Math and Literature (K–3), Book Two*. White Plains, NY: Math Solutions Publications.

This book presents math lessons based on twenty-one children's books that involve children in graphing, logic, using number sense, estimating, and working with shapes. Like the first Math and Literature *book, it is based on the premise that children learn best when they are actively engaged in mathematics. For each book, there are suggestions about how to introduce it, bring out the mathematics in it, and raise mathematical questions that will challenge children.*

Whitin, D., and Sandra Wilde. 1992. *Read Any Good Math Lately?* Portsmouth, NH: Heinemann.

The mathematical themes of children's books include an impressive array of topics, such as place value, estimation geometry, fractions, measurement, and sorting and classifying. This book introduces literature that involves stories in which people design quilts, cook pancakes, and even weigh elephants. It also includes notes about how to bring out the relevant mathematics in each story, along with a complete bibliography.

Books and Magazines for Younger Children

There are many good counting books for primary grade children. Your local library may even have a separate section for these books. I'm making only a few suggestions here.

Anno, Mitsumaa. 1982. *Anno's Math Games*. New York: Philomel Books.
Anno, Mitsumaa. 1983. *Anno's Mysterious Multiplying Jar*. New York: Philomel Books.

The "Anno" series of mathematical picture books, all written by Mitsumaa Anno, have few words but revolve around interesting stories and situations. The "math games" involve comparing, classifying, measuring, and subtracting. The "multiplying jar" is a wonderful story based on objects inside of other objects. It is fascinating to children who are compelled to keep track of the number of objects each time a new revelation is made.

Grossman, Virginia, and Sylvia Long. 1991. *Ten Little Rabbits*. San Francisco, CA: Chronicle Book.

This counting book, which introduces Native American traditions, is one of my favorites for young children.

Schwartz, David, and Steven Kellogg. 1985. *How Much Is a Million?* New York: Scholastic, Inc.

Somewhat older children are entranced by this book, which gives the reader many contexts for thinking about how big a million could be.

Ranger Rick, published by the National Wildlife Federation.

This magazine presents beautiful illustrations of animals and plantlife, accompanied by a wealth of statistics that lead to mathematical questions. For example, a mother elephant needs to eat 200 pounds of food each day to make enough milk for her baby, which weighs 260 pounds at birth. It's pretty straightforward to use statistics like these to figure out how much a mother needs to eat in a week, month, or year—or during the entire three to five years that she nurses her baby.

Scienceland, published by Scienceland, Inc. in New York.

Young children who love animals will enjoy this magazine. Each issue focuses on several different animals and includes a description of each animal's "stats," such as how tall and heavy it is, how fast it runs, and how many are in a herd. A recent issue reported that a gorilla sleeps about thirteen hours each day and encouraged children to compare this number with the number of hours that they sleep each night.

Books and Magazines for Older Children

There are many mathematically based books and magazines for older elementary school children to read on their own. But remember that independent readers also need some input and conversation around what they are reading. The mathematical content of the following materials is equally engaging for parents and kids.

Burns, Marilyn. 1982. *Math for Smarty Pants*. Boston: Little, Brown.
Burns, Marilyn. 1975. *The I Hate Mathematics! Book*. Boston: Little, Brown.
Wilkinson, Elizabeth. 1989. *Making Cents: Every Kid's Guide to Money*. Boston: Little, Brown.

> *These books are from the "Brown Paper School Books," a classic math-related series your child is sure to enjoy. Marilyn Burns has written many of them. Their appeal is that they show true respect for children and their ideas and encourage kids to think for themselves. They are packed with creative activities to tempt the increasingly complicated pre-adolescent mind!*

National Geographic World.

> *This publication, with an environmental emphasis, covers topics such as garbage, endangered species, and rain forest protection. An article on the composition of landfills presented some interesting percentages: 40 percent of garbage is newspapers and paper, 20 percent construction debris, 12 percent yard waste, and 2 percent disposable diapers. It would be interesting to think about how many pounds of garbage would be contributed to each of these categories per week, after finding out about how many pounds of garbage are dumped in your own landfill each week.*

3-2-1 Contact, a magazine that parallels the popular PBS show.

> *3-2-1 Contact integrates mathematical and scientific content in articles that appeal to upper elementary and middle-school children. Topics range from the health risks associated with smoking to how driver and passenger air bags work. With respect to smoking, we learn that the average smoker spends $700 a year on cigarettes, which is enough money to play 2,800 video games or talk to your friend on the phone for 126 hours and 22 minutes. What ideas might your own child have for spending $700?*

Zillions, a sister publication of *Consumer Reports*.

> *It's fun to consider this publication's various surveys and product tests. Kids are fascinated by the taste tests, chore surveys, and product "torture tests" reported in this magazine. This is an excellent vehicle for getting kids thinking about ways of gathering, analyzing, and interpreting data. (If you did your own ice cream taste test, who would the tasters be? Which ice creams would you sample? How would you make sure the test was fair?)*

Resources for Parents

Parents have access to the same curricula, tools (called "manipulatives" by math educators), activities, and programs that teachers do. Just get a catalog from Dale Seymour, Creative Publications, or Cuisinaire, and you will find all kinds of useful resources. The only problem is that these are often unavailable in libraries, and it's hard to judge the quality of the material by simply reading the catalog. If you want to preview educational materials before you purchase them, check with your child's school or a college library that has a strong education department. Listed below are the addresses and phone numbers for the major "alternative" mathematics catalogs. Following these listings, I've included my favorite math materials—things I've used again and again to do math with my own kids.

Dale Seymour Publications
P.O. Box 10888
Palo Alto, CA 94303-0879
(800) 872-1100 Fax: (415) 324-3424

Creative Publications
P.O. Box 10328
Palo Alto, CA 94303

Cuisinaire Company of America, Inc.
P.O. Box 15026
White Plains, NY 10602-5026
(800) 237-0338

Good Manipulatives to Have

A far cry from the flashcards we grew up with, these "manipulatives" encourage children to explore all areas of mathematics. They don't come with directions, so you and your child are on your own in using them to create and solve interesting mathematical problems. If you can't think of many good problems, a large number of activity books is available to guide you. Some of these are recipe-like, however, so if you buy them make sure your child also has plenty of opportunities to explore and make up her own problems.

Unifix Cubes

Order a bucket of these cubes, and your children will do math with them for years. After seven years, we still have about half of the cubes left from our original bucket of five hundred. Besides serving as a general building material, these cubes—which connect in one direction—can be used for counting, pattern-making, and almost any kind of work with numbers.

They're especially good for working with data: when you do a survey in your family involving numbers, each person makes a tower to show his/her "data" (number of years old they are, how often they took out the garbage that week, how many times they flushed the toilet that day, etc.). Take these cubes on trips and keep track of mileage by adding one cube per one mile, two miles, or ten miles—whatever you think is reasonable. An excellent all-around material.

Geoboards

You can make one of these, but pre-made ones cost less than $5 each and are a real bargain. A geoboard is a square board about 7" by 7" with twenty-five pegs spaced in a grid pattern, allowing you to make squares and triangles of different dimensions. You use rubber bands to make the shapes. Geoboards help children think about area and fractions while they address such questions as: How many ways can you divide this board into two same-size pieces? Four same-size pieces? Can you make a triangle that covers the same amount of space as a square?

Snap Cubes

Unlike unifix cubes, these cubes connect on all six sides and are excellent for making 3-D constructions. Children can use them to make buildings, toys, or accessories for fantasy play. If you want to do more explicit teaching, a good activity is to have your child make a toy with a specified number of cubes, then write and illustrate an instruction booklet on how to make this toy. Using only the instruction booklet, another member of your family tries to make the toy and sees how close s/he came to getting it right. This is a great deal of fun and encourages children—and even adults—to communicate their 3-D and 2-D mathematical ideas clearly.

Pattern Blocks

I find these some of the most aesthetically pleasing mathematical materials around, especially if you get them in rainbow colors. They are available in wood, plastic, and even foam rubber (which has the advantage of being noiseless). Pattern blocks come in six shapes that fit together in interesting ways. For example, six of the triangles cover the hexagon, and two of the trapezoids do the same. These relationships make it easy to work with fractions and to see the relationships among them. Beyond this, it's fascinating to do different tiling patterns with the blocks and see how you can get them to "tessellate" (repeat and fit together).

Hundreds Boards

You can make your own, or you can buy a sturdy, laminated supply of ten for less than $10. A hundreds board is simply a 10" by 10" grid with the numbers 1–100 written out in rows and columns. I find these more valuable than number lines in helping children to figure out "how many more" they need to go to get to a certain number (e.g., how many more years they need to go to get to be your age). It helps kids see the numbers they're comparing. By putting cubes or markers on the board, kids can keep track of where they are and where they're going with numbers. Moreover, the structure of these boards helps children think about counting by ten as a more efficient way of moving between numbers. Besides comparing numbers, hundreds boards help children see patterns in the number system. What would happen, for example, if they put a red cube on all of the even numbers and a green cube on all the numbers that are multiples of three? Where would the overlap be? Is there a pattern?

Games and Technology

Here are a few basic suggestions from the wide range of games and technology that is available.

1. If your family likes board games, get a few mathematically based ones and play them whenever the mood strikes. Games you might want to try include Krypto, Monopoly, SET, 24, and Mastermind.

2. There are many mathematically oriented puzzles the whole family might enjoy. Three-dimensional ones, such as Rubik's Cube and SomaCubes, are equally challenging to children and adults and provide invaluable geometric experiences. Explore the puzzles at your local game store or order them through the math catalog sources listed above.

3. Be very careful in purchasing software for purposes of doing math. Most of it is drill-oriented, and while it may "motivate" your child, s/he will not necessarily be doing good mathematics. Look instead for tool-based software (Logo, spreadsheets, and data bases for children) and for simulations that involve real mathematical problem solving. Tom Snyder Publications and Broderbund are two of the best publishers of creative software for children. For a thoughtful perspective on the educational value of computers, read:

Papert, Seymour. 1993. *The Children's Machine: Rethinking School in the Age of the Computer.* New York: Basic Books.)

Math Curricula

If you're a home-schooler, a member of your school's curriculum committee, or simply a parent who wants to do more mathematics with your child, here are some outstanding math curricula you may want to peruse. I've used many of these with my own children, particularly during summers or those inevitable times when they aren't engaged in the mathematics they are doing at school. Most of these curricula are based on the concept of small group work, in which children share ideas and strategies. If you plan to work with these materials at home, it helps to have a few kids around. These are by no means all of the good materials out there, but they are a sample of the "reformed" curricula that children will encounter increasingly at school. I've also included one example each of the new middle school and high school mathematics curriculum to give you a sense of what to expect in the way of curriculum as your child gets older.

Elementary School

Apelman, Maya, and Julie King. 1993. *Exploring Everyday Math: Ideas for Students, Teachers, and Parents*. Portsmouth, NH: Heinemann.

This is an unusual curriculum in the extent to which it emphasizes and builds upon home involvement. Though written for teachers, at least half of the activities take place at home. Units include a very interesting group of activities on family history, several on personal statistics (clothing sizes, height, relationships between body measurements), supermarket shopping, and taking care of the mail. The book includes a thoughtful section on how children learn math.

Burns, Marilyn. 1995. *Math by All Means*. White Plains, NY: Cuisinaire.

This is a series of math units by Ms. Burns and other authors focusing on various topics ranging from place value to geometry to probability. About five or six volumes have been published to date, mostly for first through third grades, and several more are on the way. There are two things I especially enjoy about these units: 1) the activities are marvelously appealing to children; and 2) the authors present real stories of how these activities have been used and how children have responded. Nothing is held back, including the fact that children need to struggle through some confusion while they do math.

TERC. 1995. *Investigations in Number Data Space*. Palo Alto, CA: Dale Seymour Publications.

Like Math by All Means, *this curriculum is packaged in units dealing with important mathematical topics. Each unit offers a variety of problem contexts, such as exploring how the number of people in your house changes over a twenty-four-hour period, or figuring out how much longer your oldest relative would have to live to tie the longevity record. In addition, a variety of number games that lend themselves to work at home are included. The currently published units are for third through fifth grades, but will soon be extended to cover the entire elementary grade range.*

Middle School

Education Development Center (EDC). 1995. *Seeing and Thinking Mathematically (Grades 6–8)*. Portsmouth, NH: Heinemann.

With this curriculum, developed by Education Development Center, children do mathematics for themselves and actively construct their own understanding. They explore architectural ideas through modeling and building their own houses; experiment with patterns in bouncing balls and toothpick houses; and examine the characteristics of various number systems, including ones they develop on their own. Traditionally, middle school curricula emphasize review of arithmetic concepts and typically have students spend half of their time with drill-oriented review. This curriculum is different. For one thing, it assumes that middle school children ought to be developing their own mathematical thinking, rather than rehashing old content. For another, it gives students an opportunity to examine mathematical concepts in depth. The material is very inviting and poses numerous challenges for children that could easily be done at home as well as at school.

High School

The *Interactive Mathematics Program* (Grades 9–12)

This is an exciting new curriculum that replaces the traditional algebra-geometry-trigonometry sequence and instead teaches mathematics in an integrated, problem-based manner. It is widely used on the west coast and is quickly catching on in the rest of the country as well. The problems in this curriculum are focused around central themes involving statistics, geometry, and number. It is a rich, flexible curriculum that challenges college-bound students as well as those who will not attend college. Results of studies show that students who participate in IMP do better on SAT than students who are enrolled in traditional courses. The project has developed an informational brochure for parents, along with other descriptive material. It's available from:

IMP
6400 Hollis St., Suite 5
Emeryville, CA 94608
(510) 658-6400.

If your school system is adopting a new high school math curriculum, this one should be at the top of their short list.

Educational Reform

Mathematics Reform and Equity Issues

National Research Council. 1989. *Everybody Counts: A Report to the Nation on the Future of Mathematics*. Washington, DC: National Academy Press.

The cover of this book says it all: it portrays an energetic group of children of all ages and colors exploring the mathematical tools they will need in their future lives.

The powerful and convincing prose points out that the public has come to accept deficient educational standards and that poor mathematical performance and declining economic well-being are the inevitable results. In order to change this state of affairs, we are urged to "invest in intellectual capital" by demanding high-quality mathematics education for all children. In one of my favorite quotes from the book, educator Marc Tucker argues that if we continue to overemphasize basic skills in arithmetic, we do our children a great disservice: "Over the long term, basic skills only give you the right to compete against the Third World for Third World wages" (p. 84). The book is available from:

National Academy Press
2101 Constitution Avenue NW
Washington, DC 20418.

Sadker, M., and D. Sadker. 1994. *Failing at Fairness: How America's Schools Cheat Girls.* New York: Charles Scribner's Sons.

"While girls are staying with math longer, it is often a matter of endurance without enjoyment. More anxious and less confident about their math ability, girls perceive the subject as cold, impersonal, and with little clear application to their lives or to society" (p. 122). The focus of this book, while not specifically on mathematics education, is of vital importance to all parents. The authors contend that girls are being subtly but systematically cheated out of high quality education. From the messages that teachers give by interacting less often with girls than boys to biased testing and to the implicit messages in curricula, the implications are clear: schools are not places where girls receive an equal break. I found this book both riveting and disturbing. Many problems that we hoped were solved are not.

Assessment and Testing

Fairtest Examiner provides the latest information on what is happening with testing reforms in this country. You'll find out why traditional tests are being drastically changed in all discipline areas, and what is behind parents' and educators' dissatisfaction with these tests. Because mathematics testing has been driven by a very narrow definition of the field, it is especially ripe for change.

Fairtest Examiner
National Center for Fair and Open Testing
342 Broadway, Cambridge, MA 02139-1802
(617) 864-4810

The New Standards Project is devoted to developing new ways of assessing students' mathematical skills. It is working with almost half the states in the country, as well as many major cities. The assessments developed by this project go far beyond arithmetic and expect students to use sophisticated strategies for solving many different kinds of mathematical problems. By the year 2000, these assessments and others like them will to a large extent replace standardized tests. Will your child's school be prepared? For more information, contact:

Andy Plattner
Communications Director
New Standards Project
National Center on Education and the Economy
1341 G Street NW, Suite 1020
Washington, DC 20005.

Tracking: Gifted and Remedial Programs

You may have assumed that tracking is an accepted part of American schools, but educators are questioning the wisdom and validity of this practice. Tracking is damaging to children, according to recent reports. Two of the best books on this topic are listed below. The first deals with the damages caused by low-level courses and specifically discusses mathematics curricula and how these can be made meaningful for all children. The second addresses problems surrounding "gifted and talented programs" (appropriately dubbed "rich and lucky" programs) and convincingly argues that what is needed is high-level, challenging curricula for *all* children.

Sapon-Shevin, Mara. 1994. *Playing Favorites: Gifted Education and the Disruption of Community.* Albany, NY: State University of New York Press.
Wheelock, Anne. 1992. *Crossing the Tracks: How "Untracking" Can Save America's Schools.* New York, NY: The New Press.

references

Anno, Mitsumaa. 1982. *Anno's Math Games*. New York: Philomel.

Anno, Mistumaa. 1983. *Anno's Mysterious Multiplying Jar*. New York: Philomel.

Apelman, Maya, and Julie King. 1993. *Exploring Everyday Math: Ideas for Students, Teachers, and Parents*. Portsmouth, NH: Heinemann.

Baker, Ann, and Johnny Baker. 1991. *Counting on a Small Planet*. Portsmouth, NH: Heinemann.

Blaine, Diane. 1991. *The Boxcar Children Cookbook*. Morton Grove, IL: Albert Whitman.

Blume, Judy. 1990. *Fudge-A-Mania*. New York: Dutton.

Burns, Marilyn. 1975. *The I Hate Mathematics Book*. Boston: Little, Brown.

———. 1982. *Math for Smarty Pants*. Boston: Little, Brown.

———. 1992a. *About Teaching Mathematics*. Sausalito, CA: The Math Solution. Distributed by Cuisinaire in White Plains, NY.

———. 1992b. *Math and Literature K-3*. Sausalito, CA: Math Solutions. Distributed by Cuisinaire in White Plains, NY.

———. 1994. *Mathematics: What Are You Teaching My Child?* New York: Scholastic. Videocassette.

Burns, Marilyn, and others. 1995. *Math by All Means*. (Series). Sausalito, CA: Math Solutions. Distributed by Cuisinaire in White Plains, NY.

Capone, Lisa. 1992. *The Conservationworks Book*. Boston: Appalachian Mountain Club Books.

Corwin, Rebecca. 1994. Personal communication.

Dahl, Roald. 1973. *Charlie and the Great Glass Elevator*. London: Allen and Unwin.

Eager, Edward. 1982. *Half Magic*. San Diego, CA: Harcourt Brace Jovanovich.

Earthworks Group, The. 1990. *50 Simple Things Kids Can Do to Save the Planet Earth*. Kansas City, MO: Andrews & McMeel.

Economopoulos, Karen. 1994. Personal communication.

Education Development Center (EDC). 1995. *Seeing and Thinking Mathematically (Grades 6-8)*. Portsmouth, NH: Heinemann.

Glover, Robert, and Jack Shepherd. 1989. *The Family Fitness Handbook*. New York: Penguin.

Griffiths, Rachel, and Margaret Clyne. 1988. *Books You Can Count On*. Portsmouth, NH: Heinemann.

Grossman, Virginia, and Sylvia Long. 1991. *Ten Little Rabbits*. San Francisco: Chronicle Books.

Interactive Mathematics Program. 1996. The Interactive Mathematics Program: A Four-Year High School Core Curriculum. Berkeley, CA: Key Curriculum Press.

Konold, Clifford. 1994. Personal communication.

Love, Ann, and Jane Drake. 1993. *Take Action: An Environmental Book for Kids*. New York: William Morrow.

Lutter, Judy Mahle, et al. 1990. *The Bodywise Woman*. Champaign, IL: Human Kinetic Publishers.

Mathematical Sciences Education Board, National Research Council. 1990. *Reshaping School Mathematics*. Washington, DC: National Academy Press.

Miles, Betty. 1991. *Save the Earth*. New York: Knopf.

Mokros, Jan, Mary Berle-Carman, Andee Rubin, and Tracey Wright. 1994. *Assessment of "Investigations in Number, Data, and Space."* Cambridge, MA: TERC.

Mokros, Jan, and Susan Jo Russell. 1995. *Combining and Comparing: Addition and Subtraction*. Palo Alto, CA: Dale Seymour.

National Council of Teachers of Mathematics. 1989. *Curriculum and Evaluation Standards for School Mathematics*. Reston, VA: National Council of Teachers of Mathematics.

National Education Commission on Time and Learning. 1994. *Prisoners of Time: Report of the National Education Commission on Time and Learning*.

National Research Council. 1989. *Everybody Counts: A Report to the Nation on the Future of Mathematics*. Washington, DC: National Academy Press.

Papert, Seymour. 1993. *The Children's Machine: Rethinking School in the Age of the Computer*. New York: Basic Books.

Parker, Ruth. 1993. *Mathematical Power: Lessons from a Classroom*. Portsmouth, NH: Heinemann.

Paulos, John A. 1988. *Innumeracy*. New York: Hill & Wang.

Perkins, David. 1992. *Smart Schools: From Training Memories to Educating Minds*. New York: The Free Press.

Pollock, Steve. 1995. *The Atlas of Endangered Resources*. New York: Belitha Press.

Sadker, Myra, and David Sadker. 1994. *Failing at Fairness: How America's Schools Cheat Girls*. New York: Scribner.

Sapon-Shevin, Mara. 1994. *Playing Favorites: Gifted Educaion and the Disruption of Community*. Albany, NY: State University of New York Press.

Schwartz, David, and Steven Kellogg. 1985. *How Much Is a Million?* New York: Scholastic.

Sheffield, Sephanie. 1995. *Math and Literature K-3, Book Two.* White Plains, NY: Math Solutions.

TERC. 1995. *Investigations in Number, Data, and Space: An Elementary Mathematics Curriculum.* Palo Alto, CA: Dale Seymour.

Wheelock, Anne. 1992. *Crossing the Tracks: How "Untracking" Can Save America's Schools.* New York: The New Press.

Whitin, David, Heidi Mills, and Timothy O'Keefe. 1990. *Living and Learning Mathematics: Stories and Strategies for Supporting Mathematical Literacy.* Portsmouth, NH: Heinemann.

Whitin, David, and Sandra Wilde. 1992. *Read Any Good Math Lately?* Portsmouth, NH: Heinemann.

Wilkinson, Elizabeth. 1989. *Making Cents: Every Kid's Guide to Money.* Boston: Little, Brown.

Periodicals

FairTest Examiner. Published by the National Center for Fair and Open Testing, Cambridge, MA.

National Geographic World. Published by National Geographic, Washington, DC.

Ranger Rick. Published by the National Wildlife Federation in Washington, DC.

3-2-1 Contact. Published by the Children's Television Workshop in New York, NY.

Scienceland. Published by Scienceland, Inc., in New York, New York.

ZILLIONS: *For Kids from Consumer Reports.* Published by Consumers Union Education Services, Yonkers, NY.

index